The Bridge Across To Forever

By Jessie Nakat

This book is dedicated to the Dreamers.

I wrote this book in hopes that I was allowed the opportunity to bring people together and allow someone to feel seen, heard, loved, enough and realise that no matter what's happened to them in their life, that they too are worthy. I wrote this book with the intention to help others, to help others have someone they can relate to, To help others have someone they can connect with, to make people who have experienced trauma in their lives to let them know that they're not alone, that they didn't suffer for no reason, and that they too can overcome any obstacle that life throws at them. When I was younger I used to dream of a love so big and so bright that it shun like stars upon this earth. A love that was mutual, consensual, unapologetically itself and unconditional. I had never known this or witnessed this growing up from a young age, I did however have a deep knowing inside my heart that it existed, more than I had ever seen, even though I had never seen it. I never had the privilege of witnessing it in my home at a young age, and I wished I did because my parents deserved that love and to give that love to each other. My little child self had been manifesting since I was a child, and little did I know or realise that this intention in itself would start a journey bigger than my mind did have the capacity to understand.

Little did I know that these series of events would change me as a person and change my mind and everything that I had ever experienced. I had no idea that a mere thought could bring about a series of events and direct the course of my life.

Little did I realise that, that little girl's dream was in actuality the beginning of enlightenment. The beginning of returning home to myself, The beginning of a journey of a million steps with one single step. In every single step, in every single thing that happened to me it was only bringing me closer to what I had asked for, that love I used to dream of. I used to think it existed outside of me, but what I soon came to realise is that the only true love in this world is the love we give to ourselves, and everything else is mirrored through us, from us. Every single thing I lost, was an illusion, I never had it to begin with and every thing that left my life, every experience brought me home to myself. Within you is a light that shines brighter than you've ever known. You may forget through trauma and conditioning that it is inside of you, it may seem dark and sad and grief filled at times but it never goes out. Our true nature is of unconditional love, the light that stems from within. Once I understood this notion, I never again could lose myself, lose another, or lose anything, because everything was already inside of me that I needed and everything that happened led to that moment and made everything, the good and the bad, worth it. For now I am home at last.

I wrote this book in hopes to let any little boy, girl, or adult who didn't get the chance to be a child and whose innocence and love was taken from them before they had a chance to get it right, know that anything is possible and that all their dreams can come true. No matter what anyone says the only thing that matters is what you think. For what you think you create and if you focus on happiness and creating a life filled with love, the universe will move around you to make this magic happen. This universe is vast, amazing and magical and I followed my dreams even when I had all my own fears, I felt the fear and did it anyway. Fear just gets in the way of your dreams and requires the same energy as love, so choose to focus on what you want to create, in every single moment. We are humans beings, here to have a powerful experience and every emotion we feel doesn't necessarily spark truth, feelings visit as they come and go, and it's our job to observe them rather than absorb them. It's our job to have healthy boundaries, surround ourselves with positive uplifting people and have faith. Your thoughts really do create your future, with every thought that happens in your head, act as if we are like an artist with his brush to the canvas, painting our future and our life of what's to come. All your dreams can come true. I want every person on this earth to know this, no matter where you are or what's happened to you, you can change the outcome of your reality.

I hope you enjoy reading this book as much as I enjoyed pouring my heart with pen to paper writing it, I expressed vulnerability and I hope that this too can give even one single soul solace, on this whirlwind ride we signed up for here on planet Earth.

Xxx
Love and light

The Knowing

As their eyes met the first time, familiarity swept them both.
I've known you for a thousand years and here you stand a new before me, we looked at each other too long to just be friends.
A million times I know I'd chosen you in a million lives.
Two souls roaming in a blindfolded dance, aspiring to meet, oblivious to what they seek likes within.

There's an empty part of me that always subconsciously was seeking you,
A yearning without fulfilment until the hands of time showed me all along I was seeking my own self to be true,
You filled my cup like a priestess drinks her wine,
My guiding light, ever so divine,
When our fingers skim I feel your touch, like a thousand lives we've been in love,
Your love guides me home, to find my soul and be one with my own,
Reminding me of my own divine worth,
Through the depths of hell I lingered with despair, filling every crack with love to mend the way, Finding solace in my self through my own strength and will,
Looking up to the heavens to feel divinely fulfilled.
And then you appear so full of love with your arms out wide,
It wasn't until I was so full of light that you saw me shine,
Coming home to you now is a blessing, you see me in the divine.
Like the hands of time were an illusion and this was sent from God for me to find,
Find myself, come home back to my one true love,
It was me all along, mirrored through you and your divine touch,
They say a soulmate is for dreamers, well we are the ones who do not sleep,
We lay awake all night and ponder ever so deep,
We think about the tides of the sea and how the moon shifts them all,
We think about how love can cure this world of it's problems all dissolved,
We think about the magic and the alchemy at hand,
We think about heaven and it's beauty upon this land,
For this worthiness we find in ourselves is mirrored on the earth,
The trees and honeybees and flowers all know their worth,
Our time upon this earth is short lived at its best,
Why do people fail to see the divine essence upon this land?
Maybe they're not lucky like you and me and fail to see?
Let them sleep, whilst we reign and create magic at sea.
The ocean is my solace, but you're my one true love,
You brought me back home to myself and for that I can never thank the skies up above enough, I find myself at peace and spreading love and happiness everywhere I go, I want the rest of the world to know this is possible and to shift their karmic woes, For if they find strength and courage to see the light from all that's within, They are able to move mountains through their faith and move away from fear, My divine sense of self and your divine unconditional love,
Could change the magic on this earth and create us all into alchemists from above,
For you see this magic lies in each and every one,
Every human on earth can grasp this gift from above,
If they have courage and faith and know that love is all within,
They too can rise above like the holy wine inside of the cup of the King,
Thank you for your magic, thank you for your love,
Nothing can ever show my gratitude you saved me from above,
You showed me my true self, You made me come back home,
When I was lost away at sea for decades on this earth.

The Bridge Across To Forever

The bridge across to forever, lord please guide me through,
Shine your light down and take this pain,
Help me understand and decipher the world around me in vain,
Why should we suffer? Why are so many children hurt?
Why are our homes broken and why is there no end in sight?
How can I hold my faith in this masquerade called life?
Children are bleeding, mothers are screaming, pain surrounds us with no end in sight, will you take the throne and end it all?
Shine your light into this world, let the hate fall, may love surround and fix these walls. May your heavenly earth be guided with light,
May you release us all from this karmic flight,
Will you ever step upon this earth and raise our awareness?
Change the frequency and help shed this ungodly curse,
You're the powerful one, the one who holds it all.
Why do so many people have to fall?
Why are there so many suffering, why are so many hurt beyond repair?
Why are so many lost and so many trapped inside their minds glare?
Why do we find ourselves fearful and unhappy with it all?
Why are we lost in this pain and have yet to step into the ascensions reign?
Something has to give, these men who rule the earth.
The ones who shed their toxicity upon us and trap us to this chain built earth.
This system is corrupt and the debts keep flying high,
There's no escape in sight and not for my children and their wives?
Can we stop being a slave to the man built prison upon earth?
Can we live freely in nature with the food provided by the earth?
Can't we just abolish this slave system and the mental chains that bind?
Tell me love is the answer,
Tell me how to help others find solace in themselves and return to their power with source, show me how to help them return to love and build a crown upon their heads. How do we free this society from the pain and the lies?
How do we make them all see their divine birth right?

Love

Love is undeserving of us, the greatest gift of all.
A gift from the heavens making us rich eliminating poor,
Through our swift adjustment to seeing it seep through,
Our veins become whole and we are able to move through,
We move to the light we conquer one and all,
Beneath the surface we breathe through golden light,
Like our ancestors guide us through every dark night,
Lord let the love shine through my veins and bring me home to all your gains,
Forgiveness sweeps my soul like the sunshine brightens the day,
Love makes me whole and real and aspires me to prosper the day.

Loving You

Love is our way to guide the light,
Even when the rest of the world is living in fear, rage and fright,
To rise above and let it all go,
To not take things personally and let go and know,
That the same bones filled with rage are made from stardust,
The same bones that bleed in pain are born from love,
The same bones that have been filled with hate are from the cosmic abyss,
We walk this path alone, connected to everything but disconnected from it all,
Moving towards God's light,
With the skeletons and bones of those we've loved and lost left behind,
Both blessings and gifts disguised as obstacles and pain,
Rising from the bottom, the depths of hell,
To rise and shine without hate and blame,
The reason you shine so bright beautiful young star is the same reason they all look back... to blame you for who you are,
Because your light shows their darkness,
The pain is all they see,
To walk and set yourself free is the way to move forward with the key,
To unlock the universes' gifts and the blessings you've worked hard to receive,
You cant take the dead weight with you so leave and fly free,
The mirror that they see is just their demons in reverse,
They too will learn one day how to undo this self curse.

Thanks For The Tragedy

Thank you for my learning, I needed it for my art,
I needed it to help evolution and consciousness and see the breaking of the shards,
The shards of hate that seperate this world from the divine,
The judgement, pain and torment that is not benign.
It spreads through our streets as fear and terror plague the earth,
And we individuals rise in consciousness to help heal this world,
To learn you create your reality,
Without projecting your pain,
Is a universal God like gift to keep yourself sane,
To have compassion, love and peace for those who are suffering without the tools,
To help themselves, others or even just forget all the broken rules,
As the tides of this world rise and bring everything to the surface,
To lend a helping hand to a suffering person who is blind,
Blinded by fear hate and all the crime,
This world is full of unreason the fear cries out loud,
To raise your hand and help another as they rise from the mud,
The mud of deceit, the mud of no changes, the mud of the worlds pain,
As we rise from this illusion we gain and walk to fame.
The fame of the light, the fame lies within.
The freedom from pain is the biggest enlightenment and gain,
When will this world see that the green dollar bills don't set us free?
The magnitude of success lies in all of the healing,
The healing from pain, the healing from hell,
The healing from drama and the healing from the empty well.
The one that lies inside, digging a desperate hole waiting to be filled from Godlike unknowns,
We as humans are conditioned and we've got it all wrong,
The glory to life lies inside your hearts song.
So listen beloved, look deep inside,
Look into all you've ever known and your souls tide,
For there lies the answer to God and your freedom from within,
It takes us all to help evolve consciousness and free us from sin.

What's it your like to find your way,
Amongst the highs and lows,
Where everything feels lost and loud and always just echoes,
To find your peace amongst the pain is to feel a hollow love,
To nourish, find, feel and reclaim an entitled sense from above,
To decipher that and understand that all that shines ain't gold,
Sometimes those things that shine are just a karmic soul,
One waiting for you to enter the pit of delight to learn your own sense of self,
You head in with all three of your eyes closed,
You realise soon enough deep within that this is a prison not a home,
But you're already there invested and you've already lost yourself,
You already realise that the pain has dimmed your magic and your light,
You think to yourself in confusion how is this love that I am in?
How did I find myself trapped in a spiders cove blinded from above and within,
What will people think of me if I am to escape this lair?
What will people do to me if I leave and run without a gasp of air,
This constant circle back into fear digs a deeper hole,
You realise karma's got you trapped by the throat in a choke hold,
You look to God and ask yourself what's the answer from the stars,
Do I stay here or let myself enter God's cave of wonders from above?
Where do I start, where do I step, where do I even go?
Help me God from up above release all this pain and all these woes,
A light is shun upon your face with answers from above,
A painful moment to say the least when you realise your own demise wasn't a white
dove, You got yourself in this cave and you're the person who freely stepped in,
A painful self realisation a tragedy to your soul to say the least,
A big deceit to your true self and now you're on your knees,
Shattered from the inside out and trapped in this without graceful ease,
Little do you realise it's only a chapter in heaven's plan,
Once you hit that peak and feel that shine, the other times fade into the air,
They fade away into the darkness as you regain your control,
Your reign beings a journey home to your own beautiful soul,
Filled with unconditional love and light and free from turmoil and pain.
You will look back and see an ancient life that served you well but no longer
resonates with gain,
Alchemists we have become in achieving internal peace.
Once you find the courage to go within you'll be rewarded from the stars,
For the cosmic dust inside your lungs is waiting to burst with love,
Once you regain your own sense of self and power from within,
Nothing or nobody can tell you otherwise what to do with your one life on this spin,
The earth continues to move forward as you linger in this cave,
Move yourself to heavens light and regain your light again,
A queen of swords you give to anyone who does not know your worth,
You tell those karmic souls to linger and you find yourself a heaven on earth,
Your power is in its true form once more,
You realise that all along this was part of the plan to bring you closer to heavens
door, You find your peace and align with your higher self,
Gifted with the divine blessings from the universe once more,

If you only knew the light that shun from within,
You'd free yourself from any karma and anyone who sinned.
The moment I laid eyes on you I knew my heart was yours,
You felt familiar, felt like I'd known you, felt like I was home after all.
You walked up to me, looked me in the eyes, you felt the same as me,
But instead you pulled away scared and more afraid than me,
You knew what I felt, you felt it too, felt the depths of the flame,
Like everything you'd ever known before was mighty lame.
This depth of love I'd never seen and never felt so quick,
But in your fear and your almighty right, you pretended you didn't and you ran away so quick,
You let fear fill every cell of your heart, you let it dictate our future and it pushed us apart. In that moment, that single moment, I already knew,
The greatest and most tragic fear of my life had just risen a new.
It took an age to forget you, a lifetime to dream you away,
And still sometimes I find myself in this lucid alternative plane,
Where you visit me and tell me that you've made a big mistake,
You realise now nothing compares and you're willing to risk take,
You've already promised yourself and your love to someone else that's new,
And you know deep down that nothing could ever compare to me and you,
I know that God has shown you now what you completely failed to see,
That I was the one all along and you ran without grace and with ease.
What am I supposed to do with your words now, do I believe everything you say?
Are you here to break my heart again or take all the pain away?
Time has shown me my worth and now what I know to be true,
Is that I deserve a love as deep as the ocean and not a shallow pool.
Not somewhere you go to feel this tiny glow,
But somewhere to shine and feel so safe and call this place my home.
For I am a queen at heart and only desire a king,
Do not touch my soul with your dirty hands, unless this is your plan,
To come forward, come inside and show me who you are,
To let down the walls to your soul and help fix any scars,
Know my worth and know yours too and choose the higher plane,
Because between us both my darling, we know that this love is insane.

Divine Feminine

My mother, why are you crying?
Wipe those tears and raise your chin, let this pain flow out of your eyes.
You are born of unconditional love and light, don't you see your worth?
Don't you know your bones are made from God?
We will rise through this chaos. We will merge through this earth together holding
hands. Walk the path of least resistance with our face to the sun, my sweet mother,
Please don't cry. Wipe your tears and learn to fly.
Rise from the ashes and let this pain be swept into the winds of despair,
The winds of hope have been abolished from this house of horrors,
The winds of hope will one day re-touch our skin,
Cleansing our auras from all this sin,
Working us through the pain towards the light,
By grace through faith and without fight,
Those things you experienced were merely lessons not luggage,
They were meant to help you find your worth and rise from the wreckage,
They were meant to teach you that all along you could fly,
Spread your angel wings and fly into the night,
The stress, the anxiety, the trauma, the fear,
Can't you just release it all into the abyss?
Can't you rise from this rubble and see yourself in plain sight?
A gift from the heavens was freedom and love from the night,
The moon shines bright and it shows you your worth,
If it can shift the tides of the sea, it surely can move heaven and earth,
For you to see your worth and know yourself deep into the night,
For you to recognise your beauty and know you divine self in sight,
Look in the mirror and remind yourself of your worth,
Look deep into her eyes and remove the pain and all the hurt,
Open your heart back up to this universe and its love,
For this pain that's inside is no turtle dove,
Your heart deserves to conquer,
It deserves to feel love and light,
It deserves to see the beauty from within and the beauty all around in sight,
Wipe the blood from your eyes and the memories of your pain,

Rise To Reign

Remember your worth and rise in your reign,
You're the divine seed, femininity at its best,
His lack of worth couldn't show you that you deserve to be the best,
This lesson was from the heaven above,
Forgive yourself, forgive it all and rise from the salt of the earth,
Your power is beyond what the eye can see,
A heavenly glow which will free and flee,
Flee the scene of anything that does not resonate love,
All that pain and emptiness was written in blood,
That day is done and today is the only day we have,
Rise from the ashes and remember this land,
Was made for you to walk upon wearing your crown,
Your high priestess is inside of you waiting to be found,
When you see her she'll remind you of your worth,
And your inner child will heal,
Like heaven on earth.

Thoughts Create Reality

Once upon a time a lady told me that my thoughts created my reality,
I sat in shock and horror, how could she believe it.
An innocent child, taken away from her every dream she could have ever dreamt,
Every park she could have ever played in,
Every night she couldn't have peacefully slept,
Every day she could have lived without fear,
Every day she could have lived without pain,
Every moment she could have felt love, gone.
A loveless home,
A loveless family.
How can you blame this child?
How can you pass judgement on innocence.
Where's your compassion?
Until adulthood, when the light shun, when the winds changed,
When God was made known when freedom was felt and
when life cleared the tides of the sand to show this illusion of hurt.
When the universe showed the high priestess and the magician,
When the universe opened the door to the world,
When it showed me I wasn't a victim to the hurt.
Think happy thoughts they shine out your face,
This illusion of thought being able to replace memories of horror,
slowly with compassion I surely did find that all along inside,
laid the divine.
The divine to control and manifest my dreams,
A fine line between letting go and feeling the breeze,
A line of power and a line of release,
A balance of harmony and peace,
When you surrender to all that is you regain your strength,
You begin to align with the heavenly steps,
For in this place you do see, that everything in life exists with ease,
So breathe and focus your thoughts child,
You're not in control of it all,
The universe has got you, the only thing that matters is to silence the noise in your
minds core.

Princess Of The Earth

Where do we go from here?
When you just want to disappear,
It's like you feel so deeply and you know so much,
But the rest of the world is out of touch,
They walk around with their eyes closed and you feel on your own,
Shedding layers and layers as you ascend into the unknown,
Surrounded by fear and judgement other's lives are held back,
With compassion on your own journey to find the right track,
As you shed layers earth becomes a hollow empty and lonely place,
Until you look to the heavens and you find your grace,
You find your feet and you shine bright,
To try to help others by being a guiding light,
Moving forward without despair,
Your life is still up in the air,
But with the faith that fills every cell of your blood,
It's in the letting go that you learn how to trust,
And all along you realise you were wishing for not much,
As the universes gifts are beyond imaginable touch.
To surrender to the divine of all that is,
The good luck and fortune roll in with grace and with ease,
For aligning with the highest truth is the most powerful way to exercise youth.
Your freedom in life is learning to let go,
To sway with the tides and all of the earths magic and woes,
For finding yourself on the journey through it all,
In the blink of an eye things pass and it all goes,
Be present in each moment and know your divine worth,
Child of God, Princess of the earth.

Find Your Way

When you find your feet you find your way,
Feels like a warm beverage on a winters day,
Aligning with what is and in the process of letting go,
Allowing things to magnet towards you and attract to your glow,
Finding your feet in the world so big,
As you begin to realise the universe does exist within you after all.
And in this giant universe inside of your tiny mind,
You begin to think about all the things that with you wish to align,
As you patiently wait for them to magnet towards you,
You now look down from heaven and enjoy the view.
With your sun kissed skin and your heart full of love,
Oh the gracious gifts you begin to receive from up above,
As you begin to create the life of your dreams,
Every painful day seems far away, taken by granted serenity from the prayers and
your dreams,
And it is through this letting go that you find your home,
And you feel complete all on your own,
You find magic in the tides and waves of the sea,
You find solace in not knowing and just to be,
Just to be is the magic in where it all lies,
To be present in each and every moment and therefore you'll find,
That the things you seek are seeking you too,
The things you love will magnet towards you,
And in this moment there's a new found peace,
That everything in life turns out with grace and with ease,
For worrying and yearning creates a resistance and a stretch,
A lack of faith and concentration causes fear and a lack of depth,
Not needing a thing turns out to be true,
Because all along what you needed was really what needed you,
Surrendering into the one with all that is, the divine,
Allows us to shake our journey up and rise with the tides,
Heaven's glow does really shine down,
The planes of existence are showing through your crown,
Raise your chin and look to the light,
For your eternal power and your almighty light can never be taken from within your
God given right,
You will look back and one day see, that everything that had to happen did so to
bring you the keys,
The keys to the kingdom which internally you did seek,
What a heavenly gift this travel through space and time has been to its peak.

Love Is My Religion

Love is the only religion I need,
It's what every preacher does preach.
"Look to the skies from the heavens above,
Let yourself be filled with love."
Then why is this world full of such hate?
Because everybody isn't tuning in and they just discriminate.
The colour of your skin,
What country you were born?
All of this nonsensical garbage is just being born,
And even with your mind full of darkness,
You sit and wonder why,
People hate and feed fear and continue to live a lie,
They judge others revealing unhealed parts of themselves,
When we are just one big giant race,
That needs to be held,
Love will guide us home and fear will tear us apart,
Yet our governments and media are the one who take the start,
Fear on the streets, media and socials, campaigns designed to harm,
Are we living real life or under a dictators charm?
Can they really take our freedom, can they really take our land?
Can they blow us to pieces like we don't have demands?
To stand up and rise in a world full of pain,
Is the bravest thing a soul could do and learn their own name,
For your freedom is your right,
And victory is your claim,
To rise in your power and learn your own game,
They control us out of their own hate and segregation and lies,
But together and united we will rise.
Through the pain of this world, though sudden but true
It takes a special soul to rise above like you do.
And with that last bit of faith muster all that you have,
Because this revolution needs us,
And so does love and your own demands.

Traveler

There was one day I was walking through life, travelling the seas,
Trying to find myself and find my worth and my rights,
Looking into this world to find myself,
Little did I see that all I was doing was letting the world get to me,
Trying to find all aspects of my soul,
Projecting my illusion, little did I know.
It wasn't the world that was going to tell me where to go,
It was within me, little did I know.
That the roots I yearned for that I called home,
Were already beneath the surface I just had to sit and dig and learn,
All parts of me I failed to love, I was running from years of abuse,
Years of torment, injustice and pain and misuse,
From others and to myself,
I learnt to let go and forgive the unbroken cycles of pain that was all I did know,
To move forward into a world without knowing what lied,
Beneath the surface of fear I felt fried,
Trying to decipher if faith was something I had ever known,
Trying to learn if God really did have my back or left me alone,
Little did I realise I was an eternal soul who chose this path to glory,
To rise above like a goddess warrior to move through tides and sorrow,
To light the way for others and heal this broken world,
To live without fear, rage or sorrow and forgive all that is and all that I'd ever known.
To understand the depths of hell later you are blessed with understanding the glory from God,
When the light shines down upon you into your heart, you feel divine.
Like a gift from the sky to this fragile earth,
Like you've conquered ten world wars, but all within yourself.
To help move through and rise and feel fearless and free,
What a glorious gift I was given by the age of three.
I didn't realise the magnitude of my strength, power or soul.
As nobody shared love with me and told me anything that I should have known.
To break the cycle and free yourself from centuries of pain,
Is to rise like an eagle through the skies and sing with free reign.
God is within us, it's plain to see that the little old me that looked out to the seas to find that freedom she once did seek, was just a broken hearted girl trying to get free.

Dimensions

To find that time and space where there is something in between,
A glimmer of hope, a flicker of gold, is time really obscene?
This illusion we cling to every day where we hurry to get to where we need to be,
When time doesn't really exist then why are we brought to our knees?
We rush around all day long like there's so much to achieve,
But where is the stillness, when do you stop and when do you just breathe?
When do you just realise that you aren't here just like a mortal disease,
And you are so much more than that, a God-like alchemist at the very least.
When you take a moment to sit in its present and see the birds and bees,
You begin to marvel at creation and smell all of the trees,
What did we do to deserve your breath and to aid our life with ease?
Is God really that great, that he gave us everything we need?
All this money, all these illusions, all these things we don't truly need,
People chase their whole life,
Like there's nothing else that would help them succeed.
Find your freedom, find your peace and free your mind from disease,
The beauty of creation, unconditional love and peace is truely the thing that will appease.

Nature

To find yourself amongst the blossom of the trees,
To lose your heroes journey as the time has passed by,
You look back and wonder how it all went wrong?
To understand the next phase, step and how to proceed and the why,
You look around and realise that all along you've sought,
An outside solution, another waste of time, a projection of all sorts.
You take the time and sit with it and suddenly you'll see,
That all along inside your soul lies freedom from within,
You realise you are the sun and not just a tiny star,
You orbit from your own strength and no longer look so far,
To find the peace that you once did think belonged to kings and queens,
Now you realise that deep within lies the answer to your dreams,
To seek this gloss and sunshine soul is part of your souls dream,
To find that solace and happy place and to feel free from fear.
You move towards understanding how it all really is,
That your mind is so powerful and really creates all that's happening,
Once you hold this notion you do choose to view,
The world with love and gratitude so you can constitute what you do,
This universe belongs to the magicians who do know,
That alchemy is the holy place the one we all seek to go,
Once we find our magic touch we then continue to see,
That all the love we spread comes back to us universally.

Grace

Sit with her and let her know how much she is loved,
Hold space for her, honour her and offer her a godly touch,
Remind her of her worth even when you've forgot,
That you are a divine being, a child of God.
Remind her of all the years that are to come,
All the chances and adventures readily available to see the sun,
Let the shine fall down from the sky and onto your face,
Allow heaven to fill your body and its grace,
Remind her that she's never alone,
Remind her of worth and let it fill her bones,
Shes the only thing you'll ever love more than anyone else,
She's the one you seek to protect and provide,
And put before the rest of the world,
For my dear darling you cannot serve from an empty cup,
You need to honour yourself and fill it right back up,
Let yourself be touched by the magic of this world,
Find love, solace and faith in yourself.
For to heal this world all we really need,
Is the makers, magicians and doers filling themselves to succeed.
To shift the universal frequency and see our world change,
It takes accountability from everyone too address their own page,
To kiss the parts of yourself that you deem unloved and bland,
Is to awaken a god like sense of self and help others do the same.
So my darling child please remember who you really are,
Before they told you anything else and left you with all those scars.
You're a child from God and you're filled with love let yourself be seen,
By Heavens grace and let that face be filled with love obscene.

Unknowingly

Some days I know, some days I know nothing.
Some days I see and some days I feel and see nothing,
Letting go of what I knew, all to love what I am,
When I think I've grown and done it all, I am humbled and realise that still I rise,
I let it all flow to me as if it were written in the sky to be mine,
As if it fills every fibre of my being,
Releasing all things that no longer serve me to the ether,
I love, even when there's no reason to love,
Love is the reason.
I fly, even when there's no reason to fly,
Because life is the occasion.
Finding freedom in the unknown,
Finding your feet in quicksand,
Seeing the world from the highest high rise,
Built on a house of cards,
Foundations are overlooked,
Things turn to sand before your eyes,
You look up from the wreckage and see,
That all along inside was what you need,
All along the answers lied within,
To find your solace and find your feet.
In a world looking to escape,
From any part of reality,
A world that's scared of its own potential,
A world so full of fear that it finds itself in pain,
A world so full of hate that it doesn't remember its own name,
But finding that shine through your veins,
To remember who you are without the pain,
Is like a bird for the first time when it flies,
A feeling like no other there lies,
The peace and freedom that you seek within,
A place of ecstasy, a place where you can rinse your sins,
Through the high vibrational skies,
Through the rebirth of your wings,
It's a small price to pay for freedom from the pain,
To rise above and claim your fame,
To walk with angels in the light,
To allow yourself to therefor delight,
And bathe in God's light and exude this love,
Through every cell of your being and into the heavens above.
For to find this solace and this peace is to feel heaven on earth,
And to remember yourself and your worth,
A love letter to my younger self.

The Sands Of Time

As the sands of time do swiftly turn,
Our endless love continues to burn,
All along I knew buried deep within,
That you would find yourself on your way back to feel my skin,
To touch my soul with your bare hands,
As your journey around this world was on reprimand,
You took each turn and you searched high and low, looking around with nowhere to
go, Cause every corner you did touch and every statue you did see,
Always reminded you why and brought you straight back to me,
It's like a fear in you gut that you can't go without,
In the back of your mind you're always on scout,
To swiftly adventure all the familiar shores,
The ones you'd known a thousand years but turned your back towards,
You sit all alone in the dark in your room realising is it too late or too soon,
To run in the face of despair and towards what you now know,
Is the one true place you could ever call home,
You look up at the stars and manifest your dreams,
As the shores of time bring you back to me,
It's only a matter of time before our souls do touch,
And free us from the unbalanced scales of karma's bad luck,
On one Sunday I'll wake up and I will soon see,
That is you all along, the silhouette in my garden besides the Olive tree.

Not Of The Divine Masculine

My fathers absence was loud and clear,
His faltering ego and loud unworthiness,
Backlashed across the sky and my innocent subconscious,
Trying to decipher what was wrong with me,
Why wasn't I enough? Why didn't he love me?
His absence was from the first day,
A faltering conception in the womb,
I felt all my mums pain and her giant wounds,
He didn't hold the treasure or key to her heart,
He broke us both and broke us all and looked away to always start,
Another war in a quiet peaceful town of women who are wounded and could make
no sound,
He brought us to tears and forgot us most days,
He left us in undying withering pain,
He forgot to tuck us in and tell us his name,
His love, his wounds his beauty and his pain,
He failed to see us and failed to hold space,
He failed to love us and he failed to have grace,
All in all it was hard to see,
Self worth, self love or just a life of anything that's free.
It was hard to see him, and see the truth,
Forgive him for the pain and all of theses deadly roots,
He was hurting inside, projecting his pain,
Without self awareness and without self gain,
It wasn't until we were old enough to see that his lack of strength and grace,
Gave us the kingdom and the key,
To be free from this pain and to break the cycle in life,
To implement change with our due right,
Deep inside all along I did see that there was a knowing and a cycle of love greater
than I'd ever seen, I knew this love was greater and deep beyond what I'd felt,
I knew this love was special and would save us and set everyone free,
It wasn't until we grew up and learnt about it all,
That life isn't painful it's his projections that were,
Life is a flower like a gift from the ground,
When watered with love it will be pleasant and shine on its way up to town,
To plant these seeds of love and to see a new life being found,
This new life of love will set us all free,
Will bring to us our greatest desires,
Our greatest destiny,
We walk now with love in our heart as we have learnt to forgive it all and make dues
with the past,
We are worth more than anything he had the ability to see,
All in all it's his loss that inevitably set us free.

Pathways To Heaven

Inside these dark veins lies a golden love light,
That can shift time and space and bring the many delights,
Of the universe to fruition and right into your hands,
The freedom gifts and grace you seek,
At the tip of your tongues demand,
You're able to fly and freely whisper in sight,
And transmute, manifest, magnitude and magician to the light,
Everything that you ever did dream,
Every part of love that you ever did feel and see,
And all your greatest desires from the depth or the seas,
If you have faith in yourself and focus your thoughts, you're able to see things
clearly and see things with love and with resource,
You're an alchemist from the earth, a magician from the skies,
A woman of power and an almighty goddess at might.
The high priestess sits in her throne,
Waiting her manifestations in all their glory and their glow,
To make themselves shown and to know the real truth,
To balance out the scales of karma and set light to the truth,
With the crook and flail the kingship of the Egyptian times,
The work has been done and restored within us to balance out life and the truth,
I've always known deep down what the future would hold, a magic place,
An abyss that I'd sit on a gold throne,
A time where the war would end and their would be nothing but peace,
A love greater than the universal tide,
A love that would make it all cease,
I found this accessible paradise within my head and heart,
So too found this goddess the one with magic and art.

Returning Home All Thanks To You

In all the times It's only now that I finally do see,
That along and all this time it was always you and me,
Two split souls born from the same star,
You go this way I'll go that way and we'll be a far,
From each other's souls since we were young,
But now with the earth in revolution the time has come,
To find each other and to find ourselves,
To do the work and retreat from hell,
To find this peace and this unconditional love,
Like a heavenly scent from up above,
Moving through the physical plane and drama and tragedy,
Every time it gets tough I just think of you and me,
In a garden of sunflowers and a bed by the sea,
The oceans breeze hitting your face and sun shedding sunlight on me,
We are in this place together and we feel like the bees knees,
We know we did the work and we know we have been set free,
Into ascension the best versions of you and me
But here we stand and know all the truth,
We've learnt so much and it's time to help our youth,
The lost and confused broken twins,
Looking for solace in all their sins,
Looking to find a freedom from within,
To help them connect and love their divine twin,
They yearn for each other and yearn through the souls,
They telepathically communicate and warn each other of their woes,
They move forward into life without an end in despair,
Wondering if they'll ever reconnect or just live a life searching for air,
But little do they know the tiny universe that exists within,
Is actually a galaxy of stars that helps conspire to achieve all of their dreams,
They find themselves and they find their truth, they see their power too.
They know themselves and realise they'll work it through,
Because you cannot stop what is meant to be and you have to come up for air,
When you realise the life of your dreams is just right there,
Communicate and find your peace and speak your highest truth,
Because there's no love like twin love, its always been me and you.
Wondering aimlessly in this world can cause havoc that's your own kind of personal hell,
To look around and to try find peace from within,
Is like trying to take a bath in an empty sink,
For what we do is search outside for what can only be found within,
Or when we look up and gaze at the stars,
Our mind can settle knowing that it's not the projection of our beings,
It's the projection of our egos that misleads us into the night,
Trying to find ourselves through some ungodly holy light,
That everyone walks around with all their eyes closed,

To be hurt, treacherous and just outright cold,
They project their wounds onto people as they see,
The world through the pain of their eyes without any light to shine in,
They find themselves in wounds with no end at sight,
But all they need to do is look inside to delight,
The inside shows the flight from the heavens above,
The inside reminds us of our worth and how to trust our gut,
To help us see faith and solace through the eyes of our own,
To see the world a new with gratitude and no fearful drone,
That shoots above this earth capturing fear in plain sight,
But rather tempering perception into a holy light,
To see the magic that exists in this world is to really live,
To find peace from up above and all from within,
You find this heaven and your world does shift,
As around you are born from your consciousness,
An awakening beyond what is known through plain sight,
An awareness that takes flight and does delight,
In the magic of this universe and all that it has to see,
An awareness born and made from just a simple you and or me,
To awaken and bare the fruit of the God's,
To understand the law of attraction and employ your own self worth,
To find your world created through a magicians wand,
Like a treasure map knowing your own mallet to a gong,
The ancient sounds lingers through the air,
Creating vibrational frequencies that manifest and do declare,
An unconditional love and giant ball of light to move forward and capture the night,
Through a beautiful light and in plain sight,
A love beyond the tides of despair,
A place to call home and plant your own seeds to bare.

Forbidden Fruit

How did I find myself in this forbidden love,
It hit me like a ton of bricks,
A plot twist, to say the least,
You walked into my life like I'd never seen love before,
Unconditional, available and free from it all,
You're sweet touch and soft lips,
Your underlying stare,
The way you look at me and see my soul and hold space for my glare,
Like a breath of fresh air,
You make me feel a certain way, remind me of my true sense,
An essence of grace and Godly love,
A change from the despair,
I see your soul and your heart it moves me across the tides,
Of the ocean floor across the whole way to a forbidden paradise,
Where we change our names and chase the sun and let go of all we've known,
To become who we were meant to become and let go from this frozen home,
That says it loves us, says its there but controls us to no end,
When do we get to feel the freedom of our own hands,
Touching each other's skin and warming each other's hands,
A feeling like we've never known,
When I look into your eyes, I feel a thousand lives,
Of ones where we have met and ran away into the sunset,
Your soul ignites a fire deep within my heart,
A burning sensual paradise one we might not start,
But in this moment all I know and feel,
Is everything you've given to me has made my heart heal,
You're a breath of fresh air in a toxic space,
A peace I'd never known,
One day, maybe just one day I'll get to call you home.

Lost And Nowhere To Be Found

All along it was plain to see the eyes of the broken soul,
Avoiding, running and trying to find out a place called home,
Someone who runs across the shores of the ocean floor,
Running from themselves all along not knowing where to go,
Failing to recognise conditioning and toxic thoughts that don't serve,
Running from themselves trying to find a place to call home,
As the universal messages became loud and crystal clear,
It was all from above and evident that there was nothing to fear,
Control is an illusion the depth of hells despair,
Why don't you just surrender sweet child?
Let go of this pain, let go of this illusion and step into repair,
Let god repair your soul and heart and let love guide the way,
Let us bathe together in the holy light and let it fade away,
You're a heavenly angel on earth,
Someone who looks to the skies to shake it up and vibrate higher than most,
Your fearlessness and angelic realm,
The way you look at me,
The way you make everything reminded of its power to a tee,
You're free from the chains that bind and see your power now,
Shine darling angel, and let the light bestow,
Freedom in your heart and love on your sleeve,
You mere presence is enough to make a thousand angels weep.

Trust The Process

I love someone who turned their back on me,
Like a thousand pains lied in my heart and I lay dead inside under the trees,
Under the trees I find such a peace it's almost illusionary like I'm free,
They breathe for me and exist so I can live with ease,
What did I do to deserve something so magical really cant I just see,
That all this world and all these feelings they are beneath me,
For this world is magic it conspires to help me achieve,
Anything I do seldom want available at the tip of my touch with ease,
Everything in this world is a product of creation,
A beautiful life filled with magic and sensation,
Can't we let go flow align with God and the trees,
For in our heart lies the kingdom of peace,
Look to where the love is and help your mind feel free,
Give it no attention and turn and face the sea,
For you'll find yourself in freedoms way in love with yourself and you'll learn to be,
Still enough to realise that you have no real control,
Of what comes and goes and flows towards or away from you at all,
But in this solace and this life you'll find your soul's counter part and home,
Because when it comes and flows towards you that's how you'll know,
That every part of life is simple and meant to be,
When you loosen your grip oh beautiful one and learn to flow with ease.

Spread Your Wings

Free to land,
Free to fly,
Free to find,
And free to see,
That soul like unconditional love can be a bliss,
A freedom one has ever known,
Free from pain and free from hurt,
Free from desperation and free from yearn,
Free from the ties that bind and free from toxic despair,
Free from it all and free from the minds lair,
The one that tells you that you won't,
The one that tells you, you cant achieve,
The one who holds the all the stars in the galaxies,
It denies you peace, lies to you night and day,
Finding solace in switching off those thoughts and being able to pray,
To pray for what you want and focus on what you can achieve,
To feed faith like a daily bathe in the Dead Sea,
For these middle eastern roots,
They find solace in my heart to know my ancestors have shown and led light on the
path,
The path to freedom, the path to change,
The path to exiling ourselves from their pain,
That we once were conditioned with since we first opened our eyes,
The ones that told us we would hurt,
The ones that left us little and cut off our wings,
The ones that projected and bathed us in all of their sins,
To rise out of this and let go of the stress,
To rise above, free ourselves and choose the empress,
The one who sits within her own heart and makes her choices known,
The one who speaks her truth without judgement of being all alone,
As she knows and yearns through the wisdom and the change that all of the gifts
known to man kind lay here right before her name,
She chooses herself and finds her self love and honours her true hearts dream,
Let's go of the plain and all the poison she's been forced to drink.

Define a goodbye,
How does someone come so quick and leave so far behind,
It's like they've flown a thousand deaths all in one week,
I find peace in my heart knowing what's meant for me won't miss me,
You have come along and thrown a spanner in the works,
Like the edge of a thousand knives slit myself,
I thought heaven and hell couldn't be friends,
I thought we found a hidden treasure buried deep within,
I thought the moment that I saw you everything turned to light,
But within a matter of days I found myself in the dark,
Why would you be gifted with my unconditional love,
Only to turn away in a fright,
You left me here on my own when it finally made sense,
In a moment of time I knew the rest of my life would hurt from heavens scent.
You showed me the world and gave me but I've never seen before,
And tore it from my feet and left me here to deal with this and more,
But once again I look in your eyes and I turn my ego down,
I stop blaming guilt and all these selfish lies and see it without thought,
Thank you for this gift to feel again in love,
To know that I could feel that way has reignited fire in my soul,
There won't ever be a day deep down in my heart where I don't think of you,
But soulmates come and go and lessons too,
One day I'll wish upon a star and name it after you,
No one even knows your name but in my heart I do.
The tears keep streaming down my face,
My hand on my lungs,
Praying for peace and a mild escape,
Thinking of sweet nothings all to get by and drown out the sound,
Of how a million times my heart has broken knowing you're no where to be found,
You showed your face and loved me hard and left me with despair,
Of the thoughts and dreams and painful nights where I could gasp for air,
Thinking of how what I felt was deeper than most could ever know,
She looks at you not the way that I do, but it suits you just fine,
Because you'll never see what I see, your worth,
And that's her favourite crime,
To treat you average and let you suffer under her fingers charm,
I sit at home and wonder why I care about you enough to try and save you from her harm,
I remember then that I am not the one that you chose,
I freeze, I cross my heart and I hope, that,
There will come a time and day where you will remember what we had,
When you finally see your worth and you know what you had lacked,
In this gift I see myself rise,
Into the hierarchy of goddess mode, to elevate and take pride,
In my own sense of self without needing to save you, I finally choose me,
I'll let you go and let you drown in the pits of the deep blue sea,
You left me here and didn't show me what I knew was true,
You helped me come home to myself and forget you.

Goddess Sea Bound

Your name is soft and special like a golden goddess ruling under the sea,
Your lips are soft and tender like a sweet little baby,
Your round soft cheeks, your soft sweet voice and your ability to swoop me in,
The way you hold your face and your tone and control me with every word,
You don't want to hurt me, don't want to harm,
Just want to see me rise,
You're like a golden kryptonite,
You make me feel a love like I've never felt inside,
The one that makes you wanna rush home and forget everything and more,
The one that lays beside you and stares into your eyes forever more,
Names your kids after cities and plays music outside,
Sit under the stars and find yourself a little too happy to care,
That nothing else in the world matters except whatever you despair,
I want to teleport to you,
Find you wherever you are,
And remind you that every day I'll lay beside you and start conversations about how amazing you are,
The mere fact that you exist reminds me that it's true,
That I am so lucky and that there is magic in this world because of you,
I become a hopeless romantic like a child at the fair,
Searching endlessly for a chocolate top ice cream before he gasps for air,
He looks it dead in the eye and remembers how lucky he is,
Right before he leans right in and gives it a giant kiss,
This is what I think of when I think of you,
A lucky dip for sure,
That the heavens above chose me for you to adore,
One day when we get to smell the roses on the trees,
I'll tell you everyday how lucky I am to have you,
Like you're the bees knees.

A Transformation Named Desire

Desire is a strange demise,
It takes you out of centre and into the pits of a place of lights,
Toys, dreams and cars, a place where there's no rules and it fills your soul,
With falsified truths taking you away from all you've ever known,
Helping you leave reality and not face the undying truths,
That deep inside of you something does lack,
There's pain, there's grief and a whole lack of solid tact,
Why is it that we think these things will change us or help us to grow?
Why is it that we think these things like capitalism and materialism will help us
show, Show others our superiority, Show others our lack of pain,
Show others all these things that seem to have financial gain,
All these shiny things that don't mean nothing at all,
All these expensive escapes,
All that glitters ain't gold,
What's in your heart finds it's way to be told,
The story will come forward and one day you'll see,
All these other things are just temporary.
Come home to yourself dear soul,
Find the parts of you that need to be held,
All the pieces that you deem to be broke,
All those pieces that could leave an army unspoken,
This beauty inside you is where the truth really lies,
All this freedom in your soul is dying to expose,
Itself and run will in the world of your dreams,
Against all the odds and the way our society functions,
I don't live a capitalisation dream,
I want to have my toes touch every beaches sand,
I want to feel the winds of the Dead Sea against my hands,
I want to feel freedom and fly higher than most have soared,
I want to see the beauty of life through a different lens,
So face the parts of you that you run so far from,
Allow the sun to kiss your skin and heal your soul,
Because enlightenment is a painful turn,
But stops the one that hurts the most,
The one of lack of self acceptance where you run and chase things that mean
none,
Let go of the materialistic dream and find the one inside your child's hands,
The one where she stops and no longer screams out demands.

Curiosity

I asked my mother one day if she was okay,
I felt her rather anxious and feeling all sorts of grey,
I asked her if she had anxiety and she said never to this day,
I looked her in the eyes and realised she'd never known she had,
Experienced the pain of a thousand swords,
Flying through her skin and tearing her vocal chords,
She'd never stopped to see besides helping the rest of the world and that
something inside her lacked and needed help,
She never sat with herself and felt the pain she ignored,
To heal, move forward and repair herself,
I told her of her beauty,
I told her of her worth,
Despite not a single person before recognising both,
She said she knew deep inside she's worth a bullion of Gold,
But nobody she'd met before was on her level and expressed themselves,
Nobody had met her match and she'd spent her life at sea,
Just searching for something not even sure if it exists,
I told her to sit with it and she will one day find an abyss,
One which nobody could take or replace,
A burning flame within that will never be extinguished,
When she found this secret place, I asked her to tell others of her finds,
Help them find their peace and spread the word around,
We are born healers from our ancestors womb,
Here to change the tides and help the flowers bloom,
I love you sweet mother now you know your worth,
Tell your other daughters that roam this earth.

Loss

Today's the day I got the call,
Like I knew the rest of my life would be torn,
I sat in the car frozen and numb,
Not knowing how to escape or what had begun,
Losing a parent feels like your house falls down and the foundations are soft,
And there's no where to run,
There is no where to hide it's all out of control,
You feel like you've been eliminated off the map and don't you know,
Day one is the worst, an ache beyond hell,
Laying on concrete bare in my front yard hard as a shell,
Crying up an age of tears, some without no sound,
The others howling loud enough to make an earthquake towards us bound,
Someone ran outside to help me with the pain,
But she couldn't hold my lungs, heart and grief from me,
She couldn't take it all away and figure this out,
She couldn't let me leave and burn this house down,
All these memories all this grief,
Much to my despair,
Nothing could ever take away the fact that you're no longer there,
When I walk into the house and walk into your room,
Empty and shadows like the flowers no longer bloom,
Losing a parent is like losing a limb,
An age of pain an awakening of sins,
The stars all had forgotten to shine,
That one day heaven gained another friend,
But I see you in the wind,
See you in the stars,
See you in the thousands of painful scars,
I will never not tell the world your name,
And share the stories of a lifetime without pain.
For everything we did together was the greatest day of my life,
And all those late night 2am chuck Norris sessions were the greatest of our night.
Your smile, your scent and the way you cooked our eggs,
Like a million dollar woman who spent her life as a living legend,
I wish I could hold you just one more time,
I know in heaven ill see your face, across the pearly whites.

Alignment is awareness,
To know ones true self,
To stop trying to fill the void with something else,
To sit inside your soul and drink from your own well,
To love yourself so deeply eliminating any kind of personal hell,
You're a flower fragile soul,
A glory to this world,
Only one of you exists through heavens hand,
You tear up the night sky with your freedom and your fight,
You show them how needing nothing is the new birthright,
You show the world your power by taking your own hand,
When times are rough are scary you fill up the demands,
Of your ego that hold you back, by talking to yourself and filling in the cracks,
Nothing or nobody can rid you of this pain,
The illusionary void is such a shame,
As the tides of change come for you, you learn easily to adjust,
As you come first and move your self instead of the worlds rut,
You learn to flow with the universe as opposed to force it at its lack,
You learn how heaven really works when you begin to hold everything in your hand,
You find a freedom high and might and taste all of the flavours of the world,
You're now an alchemist, a curator, a first born,
Change your self and watch how the world changes from the outside,
As above, So below,
Let go of the ego's pride,
Tune right in and tone it down let the world show you it cares,
By flowing and not forcing,
Let the universe hold your hand.

You visit me on the astral plane, a messenger in dreams,
You find yourself telepathically communicating to me,
Aloof with your intentions and even more silent than your words,
Do you think I'd give you my soul for not even a single word?
Not even an attempt to fix what has begun,
Not even a single moment where you chose not to run,
You walked away without a single thought and now you long to return,
After your trip around the world you found nothing, Just remained short,
You forgot my love, forgot my power, forgot my worth and might,
Now you want to show up on the astral plane like its your birth right,
Get out of my dreams you don't deserve another moment from me,
You don't deserve to come into my world like you didn't have a single issue leaving,
You left to dance with the devil, a lack of wisdom I see,
A generic desperation to be loved and adored,
But when it stared you in the face, you soon did find,
That you didn't seek love but rather an empty hand,
You now have spent your time feeling rather secure,
All to have it taken right from under you,
The universe works in mysterious ways to humble us to grow,
To show us where we are not free and where we need to learn,
To remind us of the errors and mistakes that we have done,
That's how karma works when you're out there trying to run,
You don't get to come and awaken a persons heart,
Only to run into the deep south without a moments thought,
You find yourself alone at night, awakened to the cries,
The long lost memories you disposed without a thought in sight,
You yearn for connection and forgiveness from the pain,
You yearn to reconnect and start it all again,
But how can I know you?
Who are you to ask for trust,
You don't deserve me nor do I date those who rust,
I can't be your sisters keeper,
I can't be your mothers girl,
I can't be anything to you at all,
I look at you so different, ripped the pedestal from under your legs,
Because it took all these years and all these mistakes for you to grow in your chest,
Forgive you, I'm learning how,
But to see you in new light,
To see you like my child's father is just something I am not sure I have the right,
I can't be your feminine divine, I can't be your lover to bare,
I am who I am, your hand was my catalyst to get there,
In all this learning and growing, I have returned home to myself,
I see my worth beyond what you're capable of seeing and beyond all the hurt,
For you continue to visit me in my dreams and show me universal signs,
Like I hadn't seen them for the last five years and asked God to help me find,
Peace, solace and change within my heart to forgive and let go,
That the only love I'd ever known was not ready for me to know.

You used to tell me I was crazy for thinking you weren't there,
Emotionally like a zombie you never even came up for air,
You never found yourself or found any part of you,
You ran deeper and further incapable of the truth,
You hurt me beyond a hurt like a depth beyond the tides,
An emptiness I had to dive in to just only to find,
The further I swam the deeper it got with no ending in sight,
You cheated, broke me and our home and had not an inch of remorse in your eyes,
You feel nothing when you dated that girl over the oceans seas,
Whilst you laid in bed at night and held my hand and pretended to be emotionally
available with me, Or the other girl you just happened to run into at the mall,
Was she the woman you asked to bare your child for the rest of your life?
You had a shiny muscle car and used it to capture the town,
All their attention was aloof and you then ended up alone,
You broke a wedge between us with your lack of care and pain,
You let me turn mad and criminally insane,
Believing every one of your horrendous lies,
Every last picture of you burned me inside,
Remember that birthday party where I turned twenty four,
You left me in the city alone heart broken and empty texting another girl,
It was my birthday party and you came and faked your way,
You have this way of making things about you even still to this day,
Entitlement is ugly on anyone, let alone you,
A sense of self is something you think you knew,
But to be straight up and spit out honesty there's no point in saying a thing,
You're so caught up in your ego and sense of self that you lack the maturity to see,
To see how after seven years you broke a girl to the floor,
You shattered her dreams and ran away with every other promiscuous girl,
You tried to ask for my hand in marriage and to have a child with my soul,
Whilst you were out running a muck ignoring any form of self,
Thanks for your abandonment and your lack of relationship,
You helped me determine that after it all,
I was worth more than you could even think,
I was worth more than thoughts and maybes and more than you could see,
Cause inside of you laid a broken soul one that you never tended to,
So stop projecting your emptiness and pain into another's world,
It's a cowardly thing to do,
Go the help you need to heal and change your world,
You think you're the one in anger, a victim at heavens hand,
But think back to the series of events that all were at your demand,
Whatever helps you sleep at night to find some form of peace,
The universe saw it all and everything you did,
Fear not from me but from the law of attraction because it really is a thing,
One day when you least expect it, it will remind you of all your sins.
I'd like to end on a good note but there's nothing to even say,
Thanks for abandoning me and and teaching me that I will be okay.

The Divine Sisterhood

She's my happy place like a gift from God,
A love like I've never seen, A freedom only known by Queens,
Love and support, unconditional touch, help and sweet baby like love,
A girl named by the fire of the world,
With the serenity and the peace of the earth,
A freedom that spells out a new type of world,
A new world birthed from compassion and forgiveness and God,
Why do you love me so deep?
How did I get so lucky to feel this great blessing?
How did you find me in this world full of pain,
How did you see my worth without it being to your gain?
Have you always been so incredible and powerful and free,
Inside even though the slaves of the mind do chain thee,
You're my sunshine on a rainy day,
You're the apple to my pie,
You're the smile to my happiness,
And the freedom to my life,
Thank you for showing up when I needed you the most,
Thank you for giving me hope when I saw my none myself,
You reminded me of my power and reminded me my strength,
You reminded me my divine wisdom and grace and my own self game,
Without pity, without hurt, without pain, without fear,
You showed up into my life and changed all the gears,
Into forward motion and into love,
And for that forever I'll pray for you from above,
You're like a dove flying free in the sky,
On the wheel of fortune you helped push me all the way free ride,
You're my priestess, my one true self mirrored in divine love,
A soulmate to say the least,
Like the sisterhood of the feminine crutch,
Even though it would be a sin to call you such,
You're such a shining divine grace and for that eternally I know I'm in luck,
That God chose us to walk this path for even a moment side by side,
Attached at the hip but without needing each other's pride,
You know your own name but I leave you here free,
Always protecting you even without your knowledge,
I love you forever and maybe even a day,
Even though we have decided to part ways,
I know you'll always remember those times that we had shared,
Like a golden box filled with love stored under your bed,
You think about me all the time,
I feel it in the stars,
Surrender now and move forward it's your time to shine.

Journeys

The journey is a miraculous place of all sorts of things,
From unconditional love to pain and deep sins,
From finding yourself to losing your feet,
From struggling to breathe and then breathing with ease,
Honouring every aspect, emotion and feel,
Honouring all the bad parts and all the good feels,
Some days I find myself lost in a dark hole,
Other days I feel above the lantern tops from heaven shining down light,
I find beauty in this sovereignty and this paradise flight,
We find ourselves caught between two worlds at sea,
The ying and the yang, the wild beauty and the beast,
It is in our best interest to be emotionally detached,
And see things like an eagle's eye view, from above without latch,
For this observation brings us great promise and truth,
And a divinity not known amongst the youth,
If we are to look without attachment and we can surrender the pain,
We let go of the hurt and we let go of the shame,
We find ourselves accepting it all,
This is freedom not known by most people at all,
For this gratitude and grace sets us all free,
To know yourself and be free from chains and to let it free your mind with ease.

Children Of The Sky

We are the children of the sky and it's music to our ears,
We are the ones who hold the kingdom and all the keys,
Some are born as rainbow children to bring sovereignty to this new earth,
A new place to be healed and filled with transformation and pearls,
We find that the pain holds us back in excruciating fear,
We find that others walk this earth without lineage and with tears,
For our ancestors guide us and they free us with might,
They help us break these cycles of pain that our parents do delight,
They create space for a new world free from these chains,
A new world free from the reign,
Or monster politicians who tell us how to be,
Who control us through their chains, laws and degrees,
They tell us that medicine is the only way to heal,
They tell us global warming is no big deal,
They show us fear and despair and expect we follow suit,
Like sheep that are moths to a flame in horror and their pursuit,
But we the indigo children do not follow fear and despair,
We came here to break the cycle creating chaos through free thought in the air,
There's a light inside us that never goes out,
Regardless of all the fear and self doubt,
We came to show the people the power of their mind,
That they can heal themselves, the truth and the earth all at the same time,
We are lovers born from God itself,
Like children of the wind healing parts of the earth,
The collective is here to make a greater change,
To embrace and indulge in the worlds ying and yang state,
We have to face the darkness head on without fear,
To change the world and fly and soar higher than the earth and its current frequency,
For here is where the world will change and hate will be gone,
Here is where the world with heal all its wrongs,
Here is where we free the chains that bind,
Here is where we find our paradigm,
Here is where life is to be found and here is where love reigns and frees us all from the chains that ground.

The long road home to enlightenment is a tricky one at that,
The one you find yourself tucked away and scat,
You find yourself in fear looking outside to heal the pain,
You find yourself lost and filled with ungodly shame,
You've been told since you were young who you are and how to feel pain,
To run away from everything and point to others to blame,
You've learnt all these sweet nothings and forgot how to heal,
How to heal your true nature and how to free your soul from painful cycle wheels,
You find yourself one day lost and alone like there's got to be more to see,
You find yourself hurting and like a jungle sometimes in your mental capacity,
You find yourself being told by the world you're depressed or sad,
But deep down you know there's more to it then that,
You're the universe in ecstatic motion,
You're a magician at the least,
You know some form of you is powerful and there's more to your purpose than this,
You turn to God for help, you ask the universe with your pleas,
All of a sudden you start manifesting dual understanding,
That what you now see you cant un see,
That everything you understood was life was really just a blinded bruise,
That you create your reality with a single thought,
That you're a product of all your feeling and all your thought,
You find yourself trying to free the chains that bind,
With this illusion of separation, disease and demise,
You realise surely and true that there's freedom in love,
That the people around you have suffered enough,
That you now hold the world in your hands,
That you can make it all happen and focus on your demands,
You let go with grace and ease,
After you've learnt to face the pain that lies inside all your choppy seas,
You know you know too much to not help the rest of the world see,
That their power is beyond the greatness of their despair,
That the world is here to hold their hand if they are to open their minds with a
breath of fresh air,
You let the world remember its power by spreading light and love,
Honouring all aspects from the divine grace up above,
Others so delight in fear and walk a darker path,
You let go of needing to save them all and spread light where it will last,
You feel a freedom in your heart just knowing you exist,
To heal this world and rid the planet of all that makes it tick,
It's time to find your divine light in a world that can be so empty and cruel,
And switch the switch to a place of magic, kindness and things that rule,
Your strength is beyond magnitude, Your beauty beyond pain,
You exist here to be magic without much more to gain,
You're a God on earth through the divine love and light,
A new found freedom lays upon you, you shine ever so bright.
Here you do delight in the garden of sweet love,
Where you share your new found tools with the heaven and children from the sky
above.

There was a woman once upon a time that I loved more than she loved me,
She saw my face like a shine upon a rivers glow,
I drew her in and let her know,
Her aura was electric it made my heart start, not stop, then go,
She made me feel like the thousand wings of an angel were around around my soul,
To lift me higher, love me deeper and go to heights that which I'd never known,
She said words that changed my life and sang songs that touched my heart,
She drew butterflies on the walls and lured me in her with her sleeve where she made me believe wore her heart,
She found magic in mundane things and spread light wherever she went,
She loved me deeper than a mountains edge and she always made sure I could pay the rent,
She felt like a warm glow on a summers day,
Higher than the highest high,
But I could not be who I wanted to be, I lacked the option to accept,
Be accepted for who I am if I were to love another woman,
This woman she was free, resembled an eagle soaring the daylight sky,
Everyday was an adventure she embarked on like she had no problem in her mind,
She was herself unapologetically and I found myself in a trap,
This trap of this person I had to be, one where I lacked,
The freedom to be myself, an image I had to uphold,
And then soared in like this magic beauty, She changed my entire world,
She showed me love without condition,
Showed me love without attachment,
Showed me how to be free,
She let her wings soar in my direction and it was as if my pain just ceased,
For this woman that I love so much has no idea that I am the one who loves her more,
For she's my once in a lifetime love, One I'll never get to explore,
She doesn't know how much I know her worth, even if she tried,
She's an intellect beyond her years, One who was sent here to help the tides
I love her dearly, my bee,
She showed me the world through her eyes,
I learnt how to fly and make my choice to be free from others pride,
I released this notion to God, that I was not accepted for who he made me,
I let go of the pain in my heart and saw it for what it is,
I am so blessed to ever find a love so deep, a love so pure and true,
Because most people just wander the earth in hopes that one day they do,
Before my eyes this goddess lied and it was clear and plain to see,
She'd come in like an empress from God and saved me with a single gesture a single kind thing.

Feelings are just visitors,
As temporary as the leaves on the tree,
Important guests to say the least, as we honour and release,
See the thing about feelings is they come and go,
They're not to be believed with all their crackers and tea,
As they come and set up shop in your head and heart,
It's okay to tell them to flee,
When we observe and don't evaluate,
We allow the shift to rise,
As we accept parts of our shadow with grace, ease and without demise,
For feelings are necessary, a balance of salt an earth,
They allow for a grand greater gesture,
One of self worth,
When we see what we feel without getting caught in it too long,
We are able to feel like a human soul,
And act like an alchemist of the Gods,
We sit in the field of sunflowers like a dreamer does,
One where we are only a witness to this life,
Free from the chains that bind and watching everything in plain sight,
With the earth in all its delight,
A bird soaring through the sky watching the world below,
An adventurer, explorer and self awareness glow,
Moving towards the feelings of where I'd rather be,
Consciously choosing how to exist as opposed to being a victim to thee,
For the alchemist does know how to move forward in the life of the garden of
delight, choosing their power and watching their thoughts take to life's delight.

An Enlightened Love

Standing strong in your own glow is a power of the gods,
Emitting your own frequency as opposed to absorbing all of those,
Those ones that let you linger,
Those karmic souls,
The ones where the chains that bind find you in a straight jacket and unfree,
Tied to a chair with your hands to your back thinking this was all your idea,
Looking back in fear and regret, we are at a crossroads,
What am I to do with this karmic soul and do I stay or do I go,
How do I breathe in my own power and find my hope,
Do I stand amongst the gods and wonder if the time is true,
Or do I fence myself in and stay here cooped,
Cooped up from my power and what I know to be true,
That there's more to love and more to life and more to me than you,
I sit back introspectively and listen to my heart,
The one that magnetises me towards the soulmate that's like art,
My own soul, my one true love I stand in my own divine,
Let go of being a creature to the devils hand,
For this place I do find myself in is an enlightened glow,
One where I choose to flow and grow, all the places I will go,
Like an explorer search beyond the lands but without searching for the shore,
As the shore will find the explorer every time and better land than he could hope for,
For the tides and the sea and the universe know the enlightened truth,
To take off the egos rose coloured glasses and look at things with truth,
You can't go back and change what's happened, only forgive and set yourself free,
Towards the universe and it's manifestations and needing nothing,
Everything is already inside of you and it's all that you will need,
You're a masterpiece you just forgot, yearning under the fig tree,
Your heart holds the key to the universe so listen to its song,
Let go of the shackles of perspective and thought, and ask to release all the wrongs,
The plan is greater than you ever could know, and more beautiful too,
For what you hoped for was merely a coin in the Trevi fountain pool.

The darkness sweeps through me,
It's swept through my soul,
Like a sharpened knife just after it was blunt, ready to cut a hole,
A hole in the heart of the animal that lay there on the board,
An innocent child waiting to be mauled,
The darkness came in the dead of night,
The moments my head used to linger without fright in sight,
I find myself swept up in this black cape of painful dreams,
The ones where you looked inside of us and took away our dignity,
I remember those moments like it was yesterday with no end in sight,
For a sheer moment of terror brings it all a flight,
Up towards the surface even though two decades have passed,
The darkness makes me feel like I'm in the moment there and it does last,
I talk to my inner child I tell her that she's fine,
She's in the future far away from these monsters that got her tied,
This post traumatic stress is something no one should ever face,
But alas the darkness does arise and it makes no real sense and has no grace,
It locks my adult mind up and shuts me down and I freeze in response to the pain,
Like the stress of a thousand widows has overcome my brain,
As I become aware that this memory is not about to control me,
I flee myself from the pain by accepting all these things,
These things and gains I have become by suffering the pits of hell,
To see the reverse side of the coin and experience freedom and to now know all is well,
I'm a care taker, a lover, I've got a heart of gold,
Even through everything I've experienced that remains untold,
The stories never surfaced I never got to share,
The injustice I faced and the painful anger that my ancestors did share,
I tell my child chin up love,
You're as beautiful as can be,
Those monsters in the dead of night I sent them out to sea,
They no longer hurt us, they no longer overtake,
We sit in the light together and heal and meditate,
We find this peace within our heart that beauty came from black,
A darkness known to not all daughters, and here we still do not lack,
We've risen like the kingdom that was rebuilt after the war,
The freedom in our heart is within us, focus on it all,
Shift your awareness back to the present,
Understand your worth,
Is untouchable despite what you feel, you're a child of this earth,
You my love are special and one of a kind,
You're here to change the world through the power of your mind,
All in all she hears my roar loud and clear,
She smiles and I wipe all her tears,
This introspection has got me feeling like I'm free,
Freedom from the chains that once used to bind me.

Breath is something that lately I cannot seem to grasp,
This easy reality of breathing that everyone else does make last,
I try to smile, try to focus. Try to get through my day,
But the anxiety it chokes me a deadly chemical gas may,
I find myself trapped beneath the wires of this pain,
They wrap around my lungs and they cause all this strain,
I look up to the sky after a day of barely being able to breathe,
I fall to my knees and beg for help and surrender to the trees,
I pray for awareness, I pray for an answer, I pray to take it all away,
When all I forgot to do in this trauma was be present on this day,
I remember myself as a visionary creating the realities at sea,
And cut out the thoughts, those ones where I cannot breathe,
I focus only on my mindfulness and center and align,
Align with the magic of source to take away these thorns from my mind,
Those thorns had cut my throat and made it impossible to breathe,
When all I had to do was surrender to the greater hand at ease,
Having faith required the same energy as fear,
But my mind overcame me and I lost control of the wheel,
The wheel of fortune wants to turn and move towards the next adventure in line,
So I let go of fear of the future and just surrendered to it all,
To this idea that there's a greater power, one who knows more,
I trust in myself and the universe and immediately turn it around,
Shifting my vibrational consciousness higher from the ground,
A lion in her den does hold the reign supreme,
Just like my thoughts in my head the ones that used to scream,
Scream negligence and negative thoughts all around my day,
Now I focus on my breath and make all the pain go away,
For that centre in my body is where I'm at home and in peace,
And live this peaceful aligned life without jealous or deceit,
I am no longer a prisoner to the past,
Every day I am present my happiness does last.

I long to return home,
There's an emptiness inside of me one that I did not know,
Until I got to taste my lovers sweet lips under the mistletoe,
I met this soul abroad as far away as the oceans shore,
A love like I'd never known,
One that overcame every bodily sensation with a depth to the ocean floor,
I found myself bamboozled by this persons aura and feel,
They felt like I'd known them a thousand lives under the lovers wheel,
They felt like home, felt like the missing puzzle piece, felt like the opera on a summers night,
They felt like a thousand romance novels had come up and a flight,
Into my heart, melodies sing across the heavenly sky,
That this person was familiar and their soul was a love that I did delight,
I found myself drawn closer energetically to this soul,
I found myself so drawn in like a butterfly to the glow,
The time finally came when I got to meet this person face to face,
My heart could hardly wait anymore in this race,
I walked towards her, smiling from ear to ear,
I was destined to show her a love known only by kings and queens,
Of the ascension into the highest frequency on earth,
This magical paradise I felt as I walked towards this girl,
I wanted her to know with every single glare and graze,
She was a true love, one from a Holy grace,
I got closer towards her and said hello, I looked into her eyes,
I couldn't even lean in to kiss her yet because I felt inundated with butterflies,
I looked her into soul, the eyes are the window there,
I wanted to tell her in a thousand languages that I loved her more than air,
I loved her more than the sky loves the moon and the sun sleeps every night for her,
I loved her more than the earth needs trees and water to grow,
I wanted to show her love in a thousand delicate ways,
Ones she'd never known, I was too afraid to lean in and risk her not feeling all this grow,
So I touched her hair with the fingers on my left hand, I told her poetry,
I told her how she was the one and everything else ceased to exist,
She made me feel like the war was over and I was on my throne,
She made my puzzle complete and I no longer was alone,
I showed her love through a thousand ways the rest of our first trip to love,
Now she resides as my queen with me as we work with heaven above,
This girl you see she changed my life, she made me see the truth,
That love is the only thing in the universe that's mirrored into existence and she was living proof.

Coming home to you was like a weird dream,
All cooped up in your arms feeling so serene,
I tried so hard to find my breath,
But I lost it when my heart skipped ten beats,
The way your hair curls in the sun, the light down your spine,
The way you looked across the train tracks to see me down the line,
You ran towards me like we'd waited a thousand lives to get to this,
Like every sweet touch and every soft kiss,
Was waiting for me at the finish line, into your arms,
I realised when I got there this is why,
Nothing before ever made sense and no other shoe did fit,
Because the rest of my life was waiting for this,
This feeling of coming home, this feeling of joy,
Like a small child seeing the ocean for the first time with his first toy,
I took a deep breath in and looked into your eyes,
They told me stories from years before,
Ones where you needs were unmet and your love never matched,
Ones where your hurt prospered and your joy lacked,
I looked into your eyes and I said to you strong,
All that is behind you and now it's gone,
I see your soul, I want to touch your wounds,
Heal them with a thousand kisses not the sea salt that you were doomed,
You love so deep and feel so far,
Like a bottomless pit which I'd searched the earth for,
I just let go and let it all feel me,
I let your arms and skin touch my soft sweet cheeks,
I let your energy grab my hand,
It pulls me tighter and your fingertips glaze my skin,
Nothing in the world could compare to this place,
One filled with unconditional empathy and such grace,
Thank you being a light I'd never seen,
In a dark place tunnel of a world with nothing but dim,
I feel it in my soul you're the woman of my dreams,
You're the one i was waiting for all along when I was running from ease,
You fill my lungs with air and ground me to this earth.
You are the reason for being, my reminder from the dirt,
People can change in an instant moment of time,
Which is a man made illusion but not love at first sight,
For I saw it when I met you, my soul was complete,
The other half of my life had now agreed to meet,
Even though I'm already whole,
Meet me in my highest and my happiest time,
Welcome sweet darling the pleasure is all mine.

Breathe,
Breathe when the night feels like it will never end,
When your lungs squeeze tight and your chest feels hard,
When your heart feels broken and there's no end in sight,
For this darkness is acknowledged to crack open something new,
The light must enter through to sprout new life,
New life is feared and misunderstood,
For those who have yet to see, they become shook,
They become shook by this notion that you're suffering in pain,
Like something is wrong with you and send you for medicinal gains,
They offer a concoction of pills and you feel so numb,
Like nothing makes sense or matters or helps your tongue.
There's still pain in your heart but it's masked by this drug,
Where's the justice in that? How do I survive?
How do I get through life feeling nothing at all,
Fuck these pills they gave me, they only serve my downfall,
I search deeper and surrender to the universe with cries,
Where's the answer to my present and future, how do I stop all these lies,
The universe finds me in despair and answers with truth,
The answers you seek lie within your child of youth,
I ask my child to help me through this,
She cries in pain and she finds a mountain of grief,
She asks me to sit with it and support her through,
Through everything that's happened to her and help her transmute,
Help her transmute the pain out of her body and into the light,
Help her remember her worth and teach her it's her birth right,
Before all the pain and unspeakable things,
She's required to sit and listen without acting,
Remind her of her power and hold her as she cries,
Transmute the pain til she turns to a butterfly,
She will stand tall in her power like a goddess on her cloud,
Like an empress at her table with gold leaf in her throne
Ironic as she sees her worth the rest of the world does too,
They try to catch her and put her in a bubble for their own fair suit,
They are reminded she is not one to be caught,
She flies freely around this whole earth,
She's a mystery of the gods one who knows her own worth,
Who healed from her own power through the self love game,
She continues to prosper and help other queens rise,
She helps the needy in the darkness of the night,
For to rise in love and to spread the light,
Is the ascension of the God's and is the purpose of the collective flight,
As they delight into new dimensions and help others rise,
Our earth becomes heaven on earth and souls will fly,
Fly into their power and end earths blame game,
Ego and awareness, shed that thick skin,
Peel back those layers to remember where it all began.

Ego Takes The Reign

The anger that fills my bones every time you walk away,
Every time your ego takes the reign,
Every time you gaslight and project your fears on me,
Every time you find your pain it does not set me free,
You assume how I'm going to react and forget awareness, faith and depth,
All three of your eyes are closed and you're lost in the dark,
But why dear child must you make us both suffer in this harp,
We need to escape this torment of fear, and rise above to where the winds do see,
The highest of the highs and the most beautiful of days,
The lost will be found and in divine grace,
We will ascend with the masters and rise above the tide,
We will walk like heavens door step is where we reside,
The anger that you feel is a disguise for your pain,
Just the beginning of the torment that life has shown you in vain,
There's more to you than this pain and all this fear,
There's more to you than all this lashing out and tears,
There's more to you than what aggression does lie,
There's more to life than abuse and painful cries,
Just let yourself rise and see from above,
The peep hole you're looking through doesn't quite breathe like the art in the sky above,
To rise up to the sky and take in a breath of fresh air,
Let your hair down and rid this despair,
You're a child of the universe born into love,
Let go of the pain and rise above.

The forgiveness I needed to find was within myself,
For in my head I felt I knew,
I thought I had the answers through and through,
I thought I knew where I was headed in life,
Like all these plans that were leading me to my golden knight,
I failed to sit back and let life happen to me,
I wanted to control the outcome with every squeeze,
Every time I got pushed to the ground,
My resistance to life created a solid pound,
I had a lot of questions and a lot of rage,
Everything I've ever done good had gone in vain,
I was angry at this world I was being pushed down,
I failed to raise up and reclaim my crown,
In the pits of this despair I surrendered my throne,
I asked God to come through me and show me the way to the throne,
I looked him in the eyes and I pleaded and begged,
That every time I gave everything I ended up on my head,
He looked me in the eye and said back to me,
Sweet child of mine this is only the beginning,
You pain has unlocked a new way of life,
A new way which will be gifted to you without pain and without strife,
You're a child of this universe, an explore of the seas,
You're a magician inside your heart and everything you wish will come with ease,
Just let go of the outcome and surrender to me,
With this power you will be guided without grief,
You will see the tops of the mountains and heavens gates,
You will find yourself in places of power and pleasure,
With tears of grace,
For you see my child you've chosen a path,
One of which the weak will not conquer to gain peace at last,
You're the strongest soul that you ever did know,
You will soar and rise, the places you will go,
For you see that within the deepest recesses of your soul,
There's a light inside of you that many do not know,
You will shine and lead the way, for others too,
You will conquer things with grace and ease and follow through,
Your magic within and your blinding faith has led you here,
To a diamond entry point of the rest of your years,
Raise your head now child your tears are to rest,
For the abuse and pain you felt before was part of the test,
You've risen in power and loved yourself dear,
Sweet child your life now does begin without fear.

Going through life without a thought in your mind,
Is to conquer the earth and find yourself way ahead of time,
You are able to observe without taking on grief,
You're able to see this earth and plant your feet,
For fear of the future and fear of the past,
Is a waste of your imagination and a waste of the divine inside your heart,
There's a compass inside your soul that will guide the way,
An inner knowing that is filled with peace and grace,
This inner knowing will guide you to the end of the earth,
Fulfilling your soul and your divine purpose,
For if you're reading my novel and you find yourself lost,
Remember the rainbow is at the end with the pot of Gold,
Your power is measured beyond material success,
But measured in the raising of your vibration and your souls purposeful steps,
For when you walk an aligned path,
Everything will come to you and fall in your lap and help you follow your start,
The universe does magical things and aligns those with what they need,
The power of Synchronicities and the power of your dreams,
For you're the magician not the victim at hand,
Once you see the light in your eyes the games will begin,
Your entire life will fall into the palm of your hand,
Like a lottery ticket was handed in at your demand,
Surrender to the unknown in the grace of the divine,
For not needing to know activates your birth right divine.

Two Of Swords

There's a fork in the road of my life,
Not sure which step to take,
Inundated with beliefs, thoughts and whirls of pain,
If I take this step what will I conceive,
If I take this step will it help me get to all my dreams?
What's the road to take the one less taken?
Do I take the one that's paved in Gold but the door is closed?
Do I take the one that's open wide, but the darkness lingers from side to side,
I weigh my options each give me vertigo,
I move aside and let the world show me how,
I stop my thoughts and silence my brain,
I let the compass inside myself find its way to keep me sane,
I flow with the magic that comes towards me,
If its a yes then we are set to head out to sea,
Through the Almafi coast making all my dreams,
If it's a yes then all my dreams come true,
For from the day I first saw you I knew it was you,
I knew you were the one I'd end up with,
For you see nobody else was even a threat,
Because nothing could compare to your souls counterpart there in plain flesh,
Nothing could compare to the lightning rod force,
That crept through my soul and drew you closer than God,
I surrender to the power of all that is,
I surrender to the love inside my soul,
I surrender to the waves and tides of the earths pulse,
For there lies the path to the abyss,
The one where I find myself led by God and his gifts,
If you meet me one day, ascend and I'll find you there,
For what's meant in the stars will be shown by heavens glare.

Start To Day Dream

When I was young I used to think,
Think so much I could barely resonate with the vibes from the present moment in sync,
I used to try and escape far and wide from reality at bay,
I used to believe that every thought was a further process from staying safe,
You see I was never safe in the present moment when I was young,
Because there was loud noises, betrayal and weapons at hand,
There were tides and days where the noise would never end,
Even in my adult years when I hear a loud sound,
It takes me back to that place of torment and pain,
Until I started to observe and stopped reliving each moments time,
Until I started thanking my inner child,
I looked her in the eyes and I said she's now free,
Free from this pain that burns you at the seams,
Once you honour and release my child you will fly,
You will soar into the reece's of heavens path,
You will get to taste the sweet nectar of the God's,
You will be an alchemist from heaven on an earthly path,
You will conquer the sweet unknowns without a care of the ego's mind,
You will find solace in sweet things from the divine,
In order to soar you must let go of that which holds you back,
These preconceived notions of that which you lack,
Lack love, lack truth, lack all good things,
For this sensory illusion is causing damage to all your good things,
It blocks blessings when you focus on the pain,
And stops you from living a life where you reign.

Once you see the light and it fills your every vein,
It's like a heavenly dance where you find yourself with reign,
You give up on the sadness and let go of the dark,
You align with the higher truth and feel the peace like you're in your constant youth,
Show your face to the love and let it reign supreme,
For ignoring your alter ego is forever pain,
You find solace in understanding the greatest thing,
That alignment is worth every painful sin,
When you finally come home to yourself you'll understand why,
Understand each and every trivial tribune towards the peace inside,
Every single step you took,
Every single person you met,
Allowed you to slay the demons inside,
So they no longer surfaced outside,
Finding the fountain of youth,
Inside the deep recesses within,
Let go of the control, flow it out and come home to yourself dear yin,
You're a child of the embers,
A goddess of the night,
A flow towards the heavens and you let go of the fight,
You found yourself in this fearlessness and endless day and night,
Where you prosper and win and the universe does the flight,
You're finding peace all around and flowing to what's meant to be,
As you let go of expectations just manifest and be,
Your entire world finds itself within the darkness gone,
You channel the love from the seventh plane and find yourself in God,
Your worthiness and kindness does stem from within,
Reflected on the outside surface like a glow from heavens dim,
You find this place of where you're meant to be,
Like the world makes sense all at once and all you had to do was release,
Release the need to know and control, Release the need to bare,
For when you realise that needing nothing but your own,
Is the key to heavens chair.

The Glare

Some days the clouds are grey and it all feels too much,
There's pain in my lungs and my stomach is in knots,
I feel so much sadness and I stand here scared,
I'm in fear of feeling it all and surrounded by pain there's no fucking ease,
All I ever wanted in this life of sin is to find my own peace within,
Every step and turn I take another lesson right there in my face,
I find no solace no peace with all these heartbreaking hells,
These people who claim they care,
All the abuse, all the neglect all of the disappointment and all of the cosmic redirect,
How many karmic partners, how much more abuse?
How many more self beliefs to analyse how much more do I have to prove?
Why is life pushing me to the floor, why is life hurting me more and more,
No matter how pure my heart I'm finding myself exiled,
Why do I trust the wrong people and why do they betray my pure intentions?
Why is it all pain? Where's the fucking peace?
Where's the glory and gain and any of this trauma release?
I know my worth it is so high I end up on my own.
Every time I see another lesson flyby this time I choose to learn.
I release the sorrow, release the grief, release the lack to ascend,
I choose to rise above and I choose to find peace even with no friends,
For I spent my life giving and loving eternally to those,
Who turned their back on me, betrayed my trust and sent me all their woes,
It feels like I would spend a lifetime forgiving them all for all this agony and pain,
When everything inside of me, intention wise was pure with nothing to gain,
I find myself wondering how I spent time with people who were so hurt,
But then I realised I lacked self worth,
I choose to stand up and singe all of the painful past,
Hoping in the future none of this will last,
I know my heart, I know my intentions, I know they're pure too,
They just didn't sit well with the ones that didn't deserve them too,
I realise now that every person inside of my life,
Was just a reflection of what lacked in my parental relationship advice,
For you see you when your parent is unable to love you like you need,
You spend your lifetime longing for people who are unable to nourish their own self
and take care of only their greed,
They just want more and more and take and take and leave you feeling dead,
For nothing you give is ever enough and nothing you say holds tread,
You come to the well of life and try to take a sip,
But what you've realised is you have drained the well and water doesn't exist,
There's pain in your heart and pain in your eyes and you're at the bottom rock,
But choose to look up and ascend child, as the past is gone.
For what is coming is far better than what has been left behind,
And one day you will find peace and love that will change your mind,
You'll find it in yourself and you'll return back home to you,
For since birth you've been treated like you're nothing to this earth too,

You'll rise from your own ashes with the power of self love,
And realise all of these tests were to help you ascend above,
Life's not the party you planned more a roadshow of what is,
For you had no control over it anyway, so just choose the release,
Flow with it all and let it go experience the pain,
It served its purpose and now it's time for your reign,
Those who judge just reveal another unhealed wound,
They don't even know the half of what it took for you to bloom,
Things that would've broken them in half,
They will never understand the pain you had to face to rise above the shards,
So rise child, love yourself for the pain does not last,
Find your beauty now in this everlasting graceful life.

Once you see her soul and see her pain within,
You cannot un-see and you no longer see her light as bright just dim,
Her light does not shine as bright as she projects her wounds from within,
You find yourself in a fright blaming alternative things,
You find yourself in pain questioning your own worth,
Like I sacrificed everything for this and it's the worst,
I'm trapped in this connection with a karmic soul,
Like I chose her from my own choices and she's sent from a lessons curse,
I forgot to check and ask my own self was this the right choice,
I found myself running towards her without thinking at all,
I only saw the masks she wore,
The gowns that covered her scars,
The ones that led me on and to believe that there's more to her than what meets the eye,
I found myself lost thinking she's the one,
When I walked away from my divine counterpart who represented my one true sun,
I now sit here and wallow in the pits of my despair,
How did I get this so wrong? I cant even gasp for air.
I know that what I've done has damaged everything I've had,
I know now that what happened has blatantly made me look back,
With regrets and fears as I dismissed myself from the things meant for me,
But really with this divine love I can't stop, I can't do anything, I cant even breathe.
Will I ever be able to forgive her for breaking my trust?
Will I ever be able to forgive her for the one last thing she does not believe in which is love?
She broke me at my own will and I find myself unfree,
But little did I realise she's an everlasting gift,
I rebuilt myself from my own ashes and prospered into the night,
I understand that life is meant to be lived free,
I understand that love is not meant to be unfree,
I understand that the path to ascension was the road we were meant to take,
She looks me in the eyes and forgives me for my mistakes,
For love is the most breath taking connection that ever did last,
It overcomes it all and puts it all in the past,
It allows the freedom to bloom,
The forgiveness to grow,
It allows me to recognise where I failed in my woes,
It allows me the peace I do reconcile with in my heart,
What did I ever do to deserve this divine gift sent from the heavenly parts.

There was a girl I met one day,
She laid herself to me bare,
She knew within an instant notion that there was a karmic soul at bare,
She recognised the fluctuating fears that lied within my heart,
She recognised that I of all people did not know where to start,
I knew I had known her before and knew I'd smelt her scent,
I knew that the universe had sent her to help me learn and repent,
I'd only known two loves before that damaged my internal clock,
I'd only known an unwillingness to see my soul and all of my dark,
In walked this woman across the earth she made me see myself,
She challenged my deepest notions and made me yearn for help,
She made me question whether I truly did deserve,
To be seen and heard and loved even though I failed to recognise my worth,
I realised in this time and space this never will succeed,
For everything around me made sure it never did,
I wondered deeply whether or not I would take the risk and dive,
Jump head first into love whether I understood my pride,
I realised that love is more complicated because of the things that bind,
The universal symptoms of earthly cognitive ties,
Everything she represented contradicts my own,
Everything I've ever known held no space for her zone,
I chose to let her go and set her free from the chains that bind,
Otherwise I'd cage her and her wings wouldn't be free to fly,
She fell in agony at the ends of the pits despair,
Not knowing the pain inside herself from losing this breath of fresh air,
I lay awake at night and wondered what I'd done,
If I'd made the right choice when I chose to run,
But what she doesn't know is that truly i've freed her from myself,
I'll never be the alchemist she was meant to be on this earth,
I love her in a thousand ways and a million different times,
I think of her every night before I close my eyes,
I had to let her go to fly even though I'm unfree,
Even though I fall to the ground and flail on my knees,
My one true love is never meant to be,
What is this pain I find myself trapped to and do I have the key?
The key to free myself from this cage I find myself slayed within,
I guess not, guess I'll settle and live here despite the love she's got,
What a tragic way to lose her, a tragedy at best,
Lucky she understands and has compassion and forgives my regress,
My one true love has now moved on,
I wonder what to do,
There's nothing more for me now on this earth than to pretend there's more to do,
I miss the way her skin glazed over my soft fingers and tips,
I miss the way she recognised my every word and glitch,
I lay here at night finding it hard to sleep,
As I gave away the best thing that God did send since heavens now my ditch.

Tranquility And The Beast

Inside of me did lay a beast wide awake at night,
A world of unprocessed emotions that kept me at a distance from the light,
A distance so far and so deep that I knew It wasn't meant for me,
To be around other people who challenged my every need,
Why on earth do I feel the need to suffer so deep?
Why am I holding onto this pain like I don't know how to breathe?
Am I free to walk this earth away from the pain within,
Am I free to run back to myself and forgive myself for all their sins,
I am anger, I am hatred, I am lost in the pits of despair,
I see it mirrored in the universe and I cannot gasp for air,
I cannot fathom this notion the pain is deep within,
What would happen If I forgave myself and forgive them for all their sins?
A tragic notion really, a pain buried at the ends of it all,
I see this pain inside of me like a beast at hells door,
There's comes a day where I realise the end has to come,
Where's the tranquility and peace? For the beasts time is done,
A light within has begin to rise and I will no longer run,
For this light has shun upon me and I remembered I can gasp for air,
That slight breath and sweet heavens glare,
I remembered my divine self even for a split second in time,
And no longer found myself spinning to the chains that bind,
The light so bright finds myself in this cage from within,
I rise like a serpent from the Egyptian pottery bin,
I rise into the beacon of light and flourish back onto the path,
That I fell from so tragically and with no end in sight,
The peace begins to find myself in the day after all these demons I took the time to slay,
I start to see things without shadow and remember true love,
For it touches my skin like the sun up above,
I realise that love is the only way to succeed,
For its been within me this whole time whilst I was failing to breathe,
I find this love inside of me and remember my worth,
I remember who I was before they told me who I was upon this earth,
I remember and realise my freedom from within,
As love is the existential magnitude of what lies under my skin,
My freedom is my birth right, Love is the key to it all,
After all this time, all this pain, I return home once more.

Fear is a monger that haunts the heart,
A poison that we drink like a toxic sloth,
A pain that is addictive like a curse,
A trap we walk through invisible doors,
Without a lock but we fear the inside like we are trapped,
Like there's no where to go, no where to run.
Addicted to running we forget we hold the power,
To walk out whenever we desire,
We use people things and places to fill the void,
All in all not realising the power we have to kill the noise,
Help me, inner children scream desperate to be heard,
In desperate need of attention and love,
And just to be voiced and to be nurtured,
We have so much to go and so much to do,
Please wont you just hold my hand and see this all through,
But the fear dominates and leads with its conquer,
Whilst the child screams as she really does ponder,
Where do we go from here and where is there to move?
Illuminate this cycle and break this curse from the inside loot,
For love is the answer and love we shall be seeking to return,
In infinite nature and true to who we were when we were born,
Hold out your hand to your inner child and let light guide the way,
Allow the remnants of the story to dissipate and to slowly fade away.
My dear inner child don't you see that all along,
You were worthy and loved and it was them who were in the wrong,
Forgiveness is necessary because they were unable to see,
They were unable to recognise your worth because the were blinded with dis ease,
They had nobody who taught them, they had nobody to guide,
They themselves are lost amongst the ripples and the tides,
They don't know their own worth or their own sense of self,
They could not teach you or spread out heavens touch,
They were wronged by their parents and endless cycle of despair,
One which comes to a close now for your ancestors are here to guide this new earth,
They are here to show you that you yourself are beauty in a heavenly form,
They are here to show you that God resides inside you since you were born,
So drink from the cup of love child and remember your divine self,
Nature's here to guide you and angels upon earth,
Break the cycle for your ancestors and drink from the cup of love,
Learn to give your own soul nourishment from source up above,
You will be rewarded on earth with gifts from the sky,
Forgive those who wronged you, they did not know how to cry,
They didn't know how to rid themselves from the pain that was within,
Your gift on earth child is to free yourself from their sins.

Choices

There's a girl I knew who I encountered for a brief moment in time,
She changed my soul and taught me how to stop acting potent and blind,
She softened me and wisened my heart to the strongest time of night,
Like the moon shifting tides and the stars in the northern lights,
She taught me how to see my worth in my hands, The only one who knew it besides myself and my own demands,
I found her unique and beautiful and free,
Even though she felt trapped inside a lonesome caged abyss in the land of trees, I took a glance at her in a moment and knew, this person had my heart in a single eye glance and connection too,
She wore her heart on her sleeve in a moment in time, she changed my life with her kindness and her sublime,
But you see this girl she does not know her worth, for she rejects her divine self and therefore rejects the love she deserves,
She's a queen like the most beautiful can be, but this girl doesn't know how to disassociate herself from the average bee,
She's the kind that will change your life, with a single encounter and spark to brighten the day for thee,
She focuses her love on giving her all, but she doesn't give herself any of it at all,
Inside of her I see this beautiful girl to love, this beautiful child inside who deserves an encounter with love,
For this girl that I see I love more than the world, she's the purest form of heaven, she always has been since birth, nobody's nurtured her and the grass is all dry, she's been praying for holy water to help her regain her supply,
But when the water comes and the grass does grow, she's so used to the dry land she's uncomfortable with the glow,
She chooses to live in this dead land state when her true nature is abundance and infinite grace,
She's the most beautiful thing I ever did see
I just want to tell her that right around the bend, is a sunflower patch from heaven waiting for her with her most loved friends, for what this girl has failed to see is she's chosen to settle without the birds and the trees, if she would just stand and walk around the bend, there lies heaven waiting for her at her command.

Wondering aimlessly in this world can cause havoc that's your own kind of personal
hell, to look around and to try find peace from within,
Is like trying to take a bath in an empty sink,
For what we do is search outside for what can only be found within,
Or when we look up and gaze at the stars,
Our mind can settle knowing that it's not the projection of our beings,
It's the projection of our egos that misleads us into the night,
Trying to find ourselves through some ungodly holy light,
That everyone walks around with all their eyes closed,
To be hurt, treacherous and just outright cold,
They project their wounds onto people as they see,
The world through the pain of their eyes without any light to shine in,
They find themselves in wounds with no end at sight,
But all they need to do is look inside love in which they'd delight,
The inside shows the flight from the heavens above,
The inside reminds us of our worth and how to trust our gut,
To help us see faith and solace through the eyes of our own,
To see the world a new with gratitude and no fearful drone,
That shoots above this earth capturing fear in plain sight,
But rather tempering perception into a holy light,
To see the magic that exists in this world is to really live,
To find peace from up above and allow it to resonate from within,
You find this heaven from source and your world does surely shift,
As around you are born from your own divine consciousness,
An awakening beyond what is known through plain sight,
An awareness that takes flight and does delight,
In the magic of this universe and all that it has to see,
An awareness born and made from just a simple you and or me,
To awaken and bare the fruit of the God's,
To understand the law of attraction and employ your own self worth,
To find your world created through a magicians wand,
Like a treasure map knowing your own mallet to a gong,
The ancient sounds lingers through the air,
Creating vibrational frequencies that manifest and do declare,
An unconditional love and giant ball of light to move forward and capture the night,
Through a beautiful light and in plain sight,
A love beyond the tides of despair,
A place to call home and plant your own seeds to bare.

Feet

Finding the grace and feet to lead the way
Finding yourself in life's perpetual sway,
To let go now of all that no longer serves,
To let go of all the pain and the hurt,
To move towards an abyss of love,
To move towards freedom and the truth of love,
Move away from the pain that binds you back,
The youth you ponder that you lacked,
Focus away from the pain that fills your memories and cells,
And move towards the freedom from the well,
Look inside yourself and choose to start again,
Look into the pain and make it your friend,
Remind it that all parts of you are necessary and part of the plan,
That even the darkest journey hour still serves the lights hand,
For when you find the pain you find the light,
When you move towards the good feelings heaven will show its might,
You'll realise that every thought you think will manifest before your eyes,
So let the rays leave your head and the sun fills your eyes,
With blessings and hope and focus on what you want,
To live a life full of happiness and free from pain and knots,
You deserve all the magic you can think of in your head,
So imagine dear child, your future depends on it.

There comes a time in your guiding way,
Where the light will come and find you and stay,
It helps you move into alignment with yourself,
It helps you find your own balance and health,
There's nothing greater than this moment in life,
For fear dissipates and takes it's own strife,
It disappears into the dead of the night,
It falls away without a plain anchor in sight,
It moves into the dark night of the abyss,
Away from your heavenly self and gracious skin like kiss,
You move and sway towards the passion of the night,
You find yourself in faith and delight,
You find this notion of yourself deep within,
You find yourself graciously aligned without sin,
For all that pain you once did know,
Has melted away like an age of snow,
You wonder deep within what took you so long to fall,
Only to rise into the kingdom you always did call,
You move towards your self at bay,
Finding yourself under the trees you lay,
You meditate, ponder, wonder and think,
What is it that's held be back this whole time indeed?
Was it the monsters that lay dead awake at night?
Or my mind that was the prison I did delight?
For once alignment is reached it becomes very clear,
That thoughts create reality for you my dear,
If you can just think all of the positive thoughts,
You will create a wonderful haven on earth for you to walk,
For in that haven you are the alchemist at bay,
Creating your reality day by day,
And as day by day does pass you within,
Enjoy yourself waiting for your manifestations to begin,
For fear and doubt create a cloud,
Blocking anything that you seek and you'd join the realm of doubt,
Where your attention is able to focus,
Is where you will flourish in a life of hocus pocus,
The power to focus your single thought,
Can change the world entirely from all the pain you once sought,
Without even realising it is pain that you did seek,
And finding yourself wishing under the jacaranda tree,
If you're able to forgive yourself and let go of the past,
And shift your focus upon that which you'd like to let last,
Your world will change at the drop of a hat,
For everything you seek you realise wants you back,
Delight in the kingdom of love dear soul,
Free yourself from the chains that do hold,
In this moment you will be able to see,
That all along what you were wishing for was inside of thee.

Moments in time lay dead awake in the night,
Thinking and thinking causes a deep fright,
For what is within is surely reflected without,
And what lies deep in your mind is this seed of doubt,
If you're able to look at your beliefs deep within,
Focusing yourself, releasing all of the pain and sin,
This doubt will dissipate into the dark soul of the night,
It will leave your aura without a moment to delight,
It looks to you in the kingdom of love,
Trying to remember why you once were so scared and trapped like a caged dove,
For what you failed to see and recognise within,
That all along was a holy light within,
Come home to yourself my dear beloved and you shall see,
That everything you want lies in the kingdom within thee,
The golden aura light the one that does glow,
Lighting tunnels and tunnels with power and without woe,
For inside of this kingdom lies alignment with source,
A bliss known to only some men, hidden from the higher powered lords,
Inside of you for what they don't want you to know,
Is a source of light so bright you are able to glow,
You create your own reality, the life of your dreams,
You follow your hearts desire, passion, the birds and the bees,
Changing frequency and aligning all that's meant to be,
Growing deeper and soaring higher than any human has had the capacity to see,
Once this awareness is rooted deep in your heart,
There's no going back to a lack of brilliance as we were from the start,
To understand this power and to know your own love,
Right there inside of you makes you unstoppable with support from up above,
The alchemist, the magician, the gracious god like bliss,
Creates a life of magic that you do wish to keep,
It is in this magic of source that you will soon see,
If you can focus your thoughts you can create all that you seek,
For creation is at the hand of the person in power,
The only who holds the key to the higher tower,
If you have compassion and courage to seek deep within,
You will rise and flourish to higher grounds that they seek to keep hidden,
For they know their power and don't want you to know yours,
A timeless tragedy that no longer holds ground,
The tides are a changing and the universe does shift,
With everything dear child that you really do think,
So tune in to yourself and love it where it hurts,
And watch the magic that comes from this beautiful earth.

There's something so beautiful about nature,
The salt of the earth,
It demands nothing from us, it just blooms and blossoms for us,
It offers free healing, contentment and peace,
It allows you to tune in, tap in and watch yourself fell bliss,
If you can find this magic deep within the realms of yourself,
You begin to start to manifest heaven upon earth,
Whatever it is that your soul does seek,
Can often by heard when the mind is silenced under a big oak tree,
For when the mind is quiet the meditation allows,
A higher power to speak and to reveal what you need to allow,
To allow love and peace into your heart and mind,
To free yourself from this existential prison of the mind,
Everything that you need can only come from within,
Because you are your own alchemist, your poison and your remedy,
Once you realise the remedy that lies deep within,
You allow yourself to heal and that is when the magic begins,
For the magic that lies deep within the cave of your heart,
Is what will turn this world around and tear the hate a part,
If we all were able to turn inward and see,
That everything in our universe is a mirror of a deep belief,
Once we grasp this notion the ego becomes death,
The silence of the grasp of the one who has been reborn again,
For when we rise from our own ashes and we are able to see,
That everything you feel is just a deep reflection point from within,
If you can choose a better feeling or a different way of approach,
Everything will change in your favour and that hate will no longer hurt,
For it's self imposed just a distant memory from the seas,
That something external did trigger but only for you to become one with the earth and see,
That you are your own alchemist, soulmate at best,
You're the one you've been searching for amongst this golden quest,
Nothing else matters or is as important as this,
For the number one dynamic of love comes from within,
Once this self love portal is activated from the true nature of your soul,
Everything else is just a bonus on this spinning wheel we call home,
We are able to move graciously towards all the we do seek,
Knowing deep in our bones it's coming towards us quick,
Having this awareness changes it all,
It makes you migrate from fear and operate to love,
Love is the answer in which that you seek,
And all along it was hidden in your bones deep within.

Watch them love you after you love yourself,
Like the earth no longer turns for them and for only you and your health,
It's a tragic notion, An ending for ones self,
To seek external validation, A living hell on earth,
Understanding your own power changes all of this play,
Ego control and manipulation is no longer at bay,
All that begins to matter is your self worth and love,
Knowing your own power stops all the drama that earth surely does,
For when you notice your own aura, Your own God like self,
Is when the world follows suit and channels love over anything else,
For you see you a mirror, the universe does respond,
This is law of attraction, A higher deeper and lighter realm,
Anything you focus on turns up in your world,
No matter what it is, whether its coal or pearls,
So why not shift your frequency and believe in yourself?
Focus on the diamonds and say goodbye to everything else,
As this powerful notion of peace does control your life from within,
It's like a captain steering ship winning the final race of the international seas,
It's like an astronomical achievement of creating your own path,
Knowing your own sense of divine self is the only place to start,
The person who knows they're meant for greatness before they achieve,
Is the one who soars higher than the highest before him,
Even a seed of doubt will block your blessings on earth,
So cancel all negative thoughts and continue to focus on the pearls,
The blessings and magic do lie at the palm of your hand,
You can grow weeds or flowers, it's all at your command,
Knowing your power is what changes the game,
This is quantum physics alchemy all at the hand of your reign,
Love yourself so much that the universe does see,
Only magic along your path planted with flowers and without weeds,
This is the true power of a King in his reign,
Knowing his own self worth, he's at the top of his game,
Without comparison of fear and no pain to see,
That the only thing he needs to measure is his thoughts aligned with ease,
Creating his reality one thought at a time,
He manifests heaven on earth, like a member of the divine.

Amongst the earths grain did there lie,
A little girl within locked deep inside,
She looked for peace and she did yearn to be free,
She looked for solace and a deep magicians greet,
She did not realise that what was around on this earth,
Was mayhem and malice and mud of the world,
She failed to recognise and she failed to see,
That all of these projections were not truly who she was meant to be,
All of these projections were lessons to be taught,
Behaviours from others that roamed before her on earth,
Learnt from their ancestors and projected and passed on,
Making her forget her true notion of self knowledge,
Her true notion of self worth,
She went about life with these projections at hand,
Forgetting who she was before they told her who she was by their demand ,
A time on earth did come when she stopped and asked for more,
Knowing deep down within this couldn't be the be and end all,
She knew that there was a yearning for a deeper magic within,
Like the hand woven scarf from a magician's kin,
She sought high and low and asked around all over town,
How do I find this place of solace? This magic Holy ground.
Little did she realise or know to see,
That this question alone would hand her the key,
For the question itself brought about a response,
Opening doors to show her the answers all along,
She learnt and she listened, she gathered advice,
Sat down with her notes in the middle of the night,
Looked up to the sky and asked God if it was true?
That all along within her lied a deep heavenly bloom,
One that which she did not need a single thing,
Except to change her thought process and start trusting the magic within,
He nodded with grace and sent her guidance and love,
Explaining to her she was her own twin flame from up above,
She spoke to her higher self in the meditation of night,
She gathered the confidence to believe in herself as her birth right,
Soon after she forgave those who projected their rage,
Their own hurt and their own pain,
She gained wisdom and comfort in believing the truth,
That deep within her like the fountain of youth,
She found her magic and created constellations and paths,
Helping others find their magic and breaking the shards,
This lead to awareness, enlightenment and such,
A magic beyond the grace of heaven's touch,
In this peace she found herself plain enough to see,
That all along everything she was searching for lied deep within.

Divine intervention is a blessing at best,
One that comes charging in when you least expect,
You think you've got it all worked out and you're expecting to see,
Everything you're asking, the supposed life of your dreams,
What you don't understand is your power, your might,
What you're asking for is merely a coin in a palace of knight,
A slight intervention does awaken you to see,
That maybe what you asked for isn't the life of your dreams,
It's true that there's pain and a bit of suffering at first,
But once you overcome this challenge you'll witness the rebirth,
The rebirth will shift you into a metamorphic state,
One that propels you into heavens gate,
This enlightenment, ascension opens the door,
To the kingdom, the castle, the one with the Holy floor,
It is there you find that whatever you sought,
Was nothing compared to what offerings they did abort,
The next level of your life requires the cause,
The solution, awareness and self evaluation without judgement of all sorts,
Once you see your divine Goddess within,
You're able to reach new heights only dreamt about by your kin,
The familiar is no longer something you seek,
You only wish to create the life of your dreams,
You think beyond the depth of your imagination and how you can help,
Yourself and others essentially teleport,
To whatever it is that your soul does truly seek,
You're one true purpose, the one thing that magic cannot teach,
If you're brave enough to ask yourself those questions from within,
Your divine higher self will reward you deep holy glim,
Glimmers of your wildest dreams the fruit that they bare,
The wonders from heaven upon the mirrors glare,
For what lies within is reflected without,
What you seek is seeking you without a doubt,
Focus your intention on where you wish to go,
Focus on love and the Holy golden glow,
Once you do you'll find a paradise within,
Nothing or nobody will ever dim that deep Holy glim,
For it's internal within and can never be lost,
A portable paradise you've found inside your holy thoughts.

A Mermaid's Tale

Under the rigid ground of the earth,
Lied a bottomless kingdom filled with dreams and with pearls,
It's like the depth of the sea holds the treasure chest of gold,
A beautiful abyss under the pillars of salt,
This magic place was a wonder at sight filled with graciousness and a golden light,
Fantasy at best but magic at hand,
It was the truest of places, the one where you could make any demands,
That gravitated towards you without a doubt in the air,
To know everything you'd dreamt of was available down there,
And all you had to do was focus your thoughts,
Focus your intentions on that which you sought,
If you're able to shift vibration to love,
The pillars of salt would reveal what was down from up above,
A chest full of treasure it's simple to say at that,
The desire to heaven, the one which you'd previously lacked,
If you looked inside the chest you'd manage to see,
That everything you wanted you already held the key,
The resistance exists in the failure to check,
What was deep inside in this glorious treasure chest,
For what is inside the chest is the holy night,
The Poseidon transmuted into unconditional love,
For the temper and tantrums that ruled under the sea,
Could be transmuted with grace and with ease,
Once the chest had begun to rise,
The gold and the treasure would float into the dark night,
Opening the barrel to the possibility of all that is,
Being able to transmute desire into things you can keep,
For in this notion you're able to learn,
That all things your had inside you already you need not yearn,
For this love and this Gold laid deep within,
Poseidon was just a symptom of a greater deep pain from within,
Inside of this pain the transmuting lies,
To illuminate the deep dark sea with the gold of the night,
Once this magic comes from deep within,
The entire ocean is wiped from all its sin,
Poseidon does rule without his temper and throne,
He finds himself as one with the holy light of the unknown,
This light holds the power to finding the truth,
That lay deep within you since an eternal youth,
Inside this magic the kingdom will come,
The people will flourish and your life will feel as though it has just begun,
For this power and knowledge sets the God within free,
And begins to create a chain reaction under the sea.

Despair

Do not despair the pain of it all,
It may lead you somewhere you've never been before,
How do you know that the side you're on is greener than the other grass?
How do you know that in life the pain will last?
How do you find yourself in such an entrapped space,
Unwilling to look around and see the Holy grace?
Why do you surrender to this notion of fear?
When inside you lies a throne without tears,
A power so deep and mighty that it could move the earths tide,
A power so loving and worshipped that it could change the day and night,
You find yourself in this despair trapped in your own mind,
Like you don't have the power and words that contained you in this refine,
You search high and low seeking temporary voids,
When if you just look below you'll hear the pain of your child's voice,
If you listen to that child she'll tell you loud and clear,
That all she wishes for is to no longer feel this fear,
To free her is a choice, every person must make,
To free her is a divinely heavenly grace,
To help her back up and sit on her throne,
Under her the golden light from that which she shun,
She came from this magic inside her all along,
Was the key to her power and the one which she'd one day call home,
It's like a magic light we need turn on inside,
To remember who we were before the world told us otherwise,
Once we establish our connection with our higher self,
We are able to imagine a new dream world for ourselves,
In this power and this passion the universe provides,
For it is law, and no other way can coincide,
So remove the fear and remove the doubt and remove the chains that bind,
For inside of you dear child is they key to the holy shine,
You will rise and flourish and find your power within,
This unconditional love you were born from,
Not all of their projected sins.

A peaceful state is a blissful mind,
One which holds no power over your demise,
One which entangles you with love and the fruits that bare,
Happiness, joy and nothing that does despair,
For inside this blissful mind is a person who knows,
That thoughts create reality and to avoid any woes,
For the thoughts that she thinks are manifested in sight,
Like a pen to a paper, a book to a shelf in the middle of the night,
An author on his opening day at a writing festival premiere,
Delivering his creation to the rest of the world with all his care,
This is how the magic works when we create our thoughts,
For the universe is a mirror and we are the art,
We are the artists that create this space,
We can choose heaven, hell, solace or grace,
In this notion in itself it's easy to understand,
That ours minds are like magic or weapons at hand,
For why would we focus on the pain when it's manifested into despair,
When we can focus on the pleasure and the happiness that lies in there,
No matter which way we turn it requires the same,
So focus on the present and everything you want to gain,
This scientific notion is proven at best,
Through vibrational alignment with what serves your highest and all the rest,
If you're able to focus on the positive things,
The pain will subside and the turmoil will sink,
You will rise from the ashes onto your throne,
Helping others to do the same, a heaven they'd never known,
Your brain can focus on things that are magic at bay,
No longer focused on anything that serves the pain,
Forgive the past and free yourself, The present's all you've got,
You're magic and alchemy and you deserve never to rot,
For in this understanding you change the entire earth,
You raise the frequency universally and help create a new world,
We are magic, We are treasure, We are alchemists at best,
We came here to surrender to divine nature with heaven's helping hand,
Once we master this notion creation does begin,
Our whole lives begin to revolt and change away from sin.

Freedom lies in a basket within,
Only to the dreamers who hold courage that are unafraid to acknowledge their sins,
Unafraid to acknowledge their pain of the past,
Unafraid to acknowledge their traumas that they found did last,
Unafraid to look deep within their souls own,
Unafraid to seek for a greater deep unknown,
Once this place of questioning is reached,
They are able able to start manifesting answers from the outside and within,
They realise their own power and acknowledge their own source,
Like the waters of the well poured back into themselves,
They are free from the external chains of the world,
As they only seek internal confirmation, nothing from an external source,
They understand that they are born from love and that is all they are,
Everything else is just a mirror from their own dwellings and stars,
They realise that this source is a beautiful strength,
Nothing can remove this holy sense,
The stench of the past used to linger with pain,
It no longer fathoms over this holy reign,
The power to find this incredible discovery at last,
And know your own essence is why we were born from the heaven above,
We chose as souls to depart from heaven to earth,
To learn our one true nature, our divine self,
For this divine self holds the key to the world,
This true nature and beauty is within our own hearts and our own selves,
An enlightenment that can never depart,
To find this power is a place of magic and a world of art,
To understand that your mind holds the key,
Is to unlock a chamber of secrets with magic inside thee,
Inside this secret chamber you will find,
That everything and everyone on earth is truly divine,
You're able to alchemise anything you want,
Into the palm of your hand whether you'd previously realised or not,
Once you understand this notion you will live vicariously through love,
Excited to see your creation as if you had a magicians touch,
Your mind creates the life of your dreams,
All you have to do is surrender to the divine inside thee,
Break the cycle and teach your children to return to unconditional love,
Teach them their natural state is divine from up above,
Remove the hurts from your ancestors projected on yours,
Remove the obstacles self imposed titles and grasp the kingdom of love.
Magic on earth exists whether you've seen it or not,
Start believing in your power and change the entire earths plot,
For you can create a world of happiness not pain,
Tears of joy and never tears in vain,
You feel this magic deep within your soul,
You're life mission granted under the divine worldly unknowns.

A world full of pain holds no space for gain,
At times the overthinking can lead you astray or insane,
You feel as if nothing you do or say can stop,
Like a timeless tickling circling madness clock,
You realise that you're all caught up in your head,
Nothing but failures and existential dread,
Until you start to decipher all that isn't logical thoughts,
You turn inwards towards the pain and address is with all sorts,
Of compassion, love, kindness and trust,
That you will rise from the ashes far up above,
You open your chakras and open that third eye,
You listen to the cries from your inner child deep inside,
You remind her that her pain was a lesson and not a curse,
And there's magic to be found all upon this beautiful earth,
That she is a creative soul as beautiful as can be,
It's not her fault what happened to her and it's choice of her worth to be decided
from deep within,
She's an alchemist at best and her own one true love,
Like she was destined for greatness from the heavens above,
She wiped the tears from her eyes and stood up to see,
That everything she wants she deserves with grace and ease,
All of these monsters that came to slay her in the night,
We're just mirrored reflections of her deepest fearful beliefs about fright,
All of the people she trusted had betrayed her own true soul,
And now it was time to rise and evolve from the evil of it all,
She talked about fairies and magic and saw all that glittered on this earth,
She was able to realise her own magic for it was born from her own soul,
In this self transmutation she was able to grow,
Flying high into the world and the potential she soon will know,
Everything worked out for her it's beautiful to see,
That something that was born from the ashes could rise like a Phoenix ever so free.

Pain is a concept that is uneasy to grasp,
One that creates chaos and surely does not bring magic into last,
Why would we focus on the things that hurt,
When we can shift our focus to the magnificence of this earth,
We are tyrants when we succumb to the notion of pain,
Like there's nothing heaven can offer that we would have to gain,
Surrender your fears to the creator of this earth,
Focus on love and things that bloom from the dirt,
For in this notion we will truly begin to see,
The world around us shift with grace and with ease,
We rise from the tremors into this powerful might,
Like children from the sky living our birth right,
It's so gracefully easy to notice the shift,
When you whole heartedly assist your thoughts and beliefs,
To know that you deserve greatness and to see it shape shift,
Towards you in your life is a blessing only God could gift,
To know you could become any part of this earth,
To resonate at a vibration higher than dirt,
We are able to manage our emotions with grace,
And rise towards this divine Holy place,
For in this notion of controlling our thoughts,
Focusing on that which we'd seek to create makes all sorts,
Of power, hierarchy, magic and lacks pain,
We are able to begin to understand our essence on this plane,
That we are energy and we emit a consciousness in that which we can gain,
This vibration we emit into the universe,
Contributes to that which we receive on this earth,
If we raise our vibration we are able to see,
That every dream we seek will be created with ease,
Understanding this power changes the game,
It makes you realise that everything you think is created whether it's intentional or in vain,
So raise your thoughts and your vibe and you will soon see,
That solar child you're a magician to be.

Fearing your power is a disservice to man,
It goes against everything in that which you were born to stand,
You're a freedom writer, a peace keeper, the divine in your own hand,
To lose your self love, confidence and self trust,
Can happen at times upon this earth,
Not knowing which way to look or which way to turn,
You get caught up in your thoughts like they're the be an end all,
But really they're just a noise that you eventually learn to ignore,
You realise your own demise lies at the hand of believing,
Anything and everything your mind is conceiving,
You move towards compassion and self love for yourself,
Let go of all the pain the you felt at the hand of the earth,
Sometimes my sunshine got stolen by another,
Because they failed to recognise their own and used me as their umbrella,
They didn't let me love and show me love in return,
It was there i realised that this is where I did yearn,
I yearned to be seen, heard, loved and known,
I yearned to feel magic in another's words,
What I failed to recognise and see all along,
Was that deep inside of me I wasn't so strong,
I didn't give myself these pleasures I looked for them outside,
This was where my downfall began and nothing did coincide,
I realised that this fear and pain all began within,
Because my own lack of self love had started with my own kin,
They didn't have the capacity to show themselves that love,
They handed down their pain and I realised I felt nothing magic since the doctors touch,
What I did come to learn at the pain of life's hand,
Is that I can create my own magic in the palm of my own hand,
I know how to rise and revel in the glory,
That love is my one true divine and only story,
It's the essence which I came from and the essence which I will return,
The power of my own self belief,
Gave my world a magical turn,
I turned to myself and watered my own roots,
I found myself yearning for peace in places of loot,
I found a new paradise that lay deeper within,
One nobody had ever shown me or found solace out of their owns sins,
I then began to realise it wasn't even their fault,
They also had suffered at the hand of someone's else's result,
So forgiveness became my ally,
My one true best friend,
As I rose from the ashes and towards heavens hand,
I realised now more than ever that nothing else could take,
My power, my one true love, my own divine grace,
With this realisation I did now return home,
And everything around me shifted in a way I'd never known,
The universe became aware of my peace and my own self growth,

It mirrored what was inside of me and handed me gold,
You yourself are able to create this magic too,
For if I came from hell there's a chance you did too,
So change your thoughts and refocus on the love,
After all it's where you're born from and it's where you'll return, to love.

The Lost Inner Children

My fathers absence screamed itself in my face,
Always yearning for lovers who would fulfil his place,
Every man that I did ever touch,
Only left me yearning for anything besides lust,
They never saw my soul and recognised my worth,
They always made me an option and departed from me upon this earth,
They showed me their true selves but still my heart did find,
A reason to believe they had the potential to love inside,
I started to realise that there had to be more,
Had to be more than this pain and the abandonment of it all,
How were others so in love? And I was in such pain?
How were others given love and it denied to my name?
These realisations made me ache and yearn from within,
That I'd been denied a Holy right of love like I had sinned,
I lay awake at night and cry myself to sleep,
Wondering what I'd done to deserve this pain as I weeped,
I realised shortly after that intention was the one,
The one that was the catalyst to changing everything I'd ever done,
That simple intention sparked a universal notion,
To prove to me and show me what door I'd asked to open,
Every single person I did meet after that,
Was a karmic single lesson to show me were I lacked,
To show me where I was unfree and where the pain had roots,
To help me open my heart and to rid of dark ancestral truths,
One that spoke of unworthiness and abuse and conditional love,
Helping me break free from theses chains and cycles handed down from above,
Each and every person tore a shatter in my heart,
Until I finally realised no friend or lover would treat me with the love I did feel inside,
Until I was able to break free from attracting karmic souls,
The ones who linger round and keep you in a chokehold,
They show you dead of night and abandon you in the day,
They let you taste the liquor and then they flee without a say,
Every single lesson, every painful truth,
Was that nobody loved me, not even in my youth,
I realised that this cycle was one that was a curse,
That I had to break from my ancestral line of hurt,
I decided to start researching the power of my mind,
Cutting everything and anyone who I no longer did find,
Fulfilled my soul and deserved my presence in their line of sight,
Only left with myself what a lonely feeling, what a fright,
Until I realised that I never was alone,
I had the universe at hand, my finger tips,
Manifesting my command,
I could draw people worthy of me for now I'd told the world,
I'm no longer tolerating anything than a golden throne upon this earth,

This powerful message sent waves out into space,
A vibrational frequency filled with Holy grace,
This magic begun to show up at my wooden door,
One by one of a person who came bearing it all,
They showed me love and wanted me to be their guiding light,
They loved me like I deserved, finally a change in sight,
I never had a doubt in my mind that this would all come true,
But the magic really lied in my own self beliefs and proof,
I found power in solidarity, A warrior in my heart,
One that never gave up and still spread love despite all the shards,
The ones the broken souls tried to leave my aura filled with,
I sent them to creators light and replaced with a beautiful solar eclipse,
An abyss of magic fills my life I am so divinely blessed,
Only because I had courage to send them on their quest,
Now I sleep everyday wanting to show the world,
That suffering is a taught choice, and it's you that no longer has to yearn,
You're a warrior a shining light, there's power inside of your soul,
You're able to accomplish anything you can conceptualise inside that mind of gold.

Inside this new found ascension a new awareness began,
One where fear did not conquer and it did not control all of the lands,
The new found awareness brought out a single sprout,
It taught me how even a single seed of doubt,
Could block my blessings and stop me from achieving all my dreams,
If I did not believe in Heaven's grace and my own accomplishments and things,
Nobody else would recognise and take pride and notice me,
Nobody would mirror the deserving energy I did keep,
So every time I had a thought that no longer served my needs,
I imagined it dissipating inside my mind with ease,
I sent it to the golden light away from my consciousness,
And replaced with something that helped me rise to bliss,
Success is my birth right,
Success is my name,
Success is my one true purpose and next of kin,
To help this world heal and to help this world shatter their own entrapment too,
In this notion I understood the power of the mind,
The universal consciousness nobody else seems to have the time to find,
Making time isn't a choice it's an essential to this earth,
For if you're are not in alignment nothing else can birth,
This simple understanding is one from Heaven's tact,
One where you are now are able to create everything that you did lack,
You rise into your power when you take the time to find,
That life all along was something beyond the hands of time,
Time is an illusion made by mans small mind,
This notion of being in a rush only to find,
There's no where to go and nothing to do, this impending doom and lack,
Is really one taught by the masses to show you how to hold back,
Your divinity and your purpose as an alchemist on earth,
They stripped you of your birth right and you don't even know your worth,
This conceptualisation from politics keeping us all small,
When they have the answers and the keys and the power to it all,
If you are able to awaken and teach your fellow youth,
Your purpose on earth is already greater as you've been given the truth,
This nine to five rat race, this cosmic despair,
One where they try and medicate you for not thinking like the masses of the land,
They fail to recognise when you're sprouting and growing into power,
As they've witnessed this and they judge you like you're a burning tower,
But continue to rise into power and find your birth right and truth,
That all along inside of you is a magician who could control the earth and youth,
Who could help others see their power and rise from the control of the political gain,
To show yourselves your freedom and know you too can reign,
They already know this and they hide from us all,
They try and show us nothing like we're sheep living low at their beckoned call,
But what they can't take from us is our spirit and our dreams,
For indigo children upon this earth will change the universal stream,
If you're feeling kind of clustered just send it to the light and remember that this
divine grace is your heavenly birth right.

We danced close to love,
But there was a thorn in your side,
It affected and hurt your heart deep inside,
Betrayed your heavenly stride,
You found solace in the loneliness and fear within every cell of your blood,
You failed to recognise this divine love,
You moved towards your own insanity at a graceless pace,
You moved away from love and stripped me of my faith,
In this manic emotion I lost alignment with myself,
Hoping to find happiness in a place you lived in that reassembled hell,
It's a sad notion to think that you didn't want to be saved,
That you didn't care enough to feel anything besides pain,
You revelled in this pain and fear and hurt your heart so deep,
You wiped out colonies of tears,
But what you failed to see was you held the power,
To illuminate the light and remove the tower,
The one you lived in the dark of night,
The one you laid awake in feeling fears fright,
It's a sadness deep within that you failed to see,
Your pain was anything besides setting you free,
Moving away from you made me realise a lot,
That heaven is real and hell is a twisted plot,
One which you enjoy the depths of it's dark,
One where you set up roots and built a home of bones,
You failed to recognise your own power in its might,
Or even see yourself mildly from heavens flight,
This sadness lingered and webbed me in,
It made me think I was grieving all of your sins,
But freedom from the web has made me see,
That its you who enjoys the suffering and no freedom from the tears,
I built a cottage for us both, One where we could revel in the love we once had
hoped,
Sunflowers by the edge and graciously free,
I even hand picked you some tea, But the tea was like poison to your mouth,
For your divine refusal of love is where you found,
Solace in the pain, a lingering cycle,
It was me who evolved learning I could never be grounded,
In this prison you built, the one you called home,
I tried to love you so hard but you never saw,
I hope one day you open the door,
They key's in your hand and heaven's waiting for your call.

The dreams that fills every night and day,
Like being around you is some form of socialist decay,
My mind wandered why every time you sucked me in,
To your self absorbed ways and lack of happiness that you sat in,
I found out the hard way you aren't able to love,
You showed me parts of yourself that were mirrored from up above,
But what I surely came to recognise and see is that the pain was greater than you're incentive to be free,
You're a lost little soul under the wishing tree,
My love can't save you that much we know is true,
It's sad really how everything came through,
But I will remind myself on my darkest days,
That there's nothing I could focus on that will make things change,
For you've been destined well before me to suffer at the hand,
Of your passed down projected emptiness and pain,
You found a way into my heart,
But what I realised is I saw parts of myself in you from the start,
Maybe it was me who was yearning for your love,
To free the parts of myself that I saw inside of you that were still in my heart,
You realise now that you'll never be free,
What a trapped notion to live inside thee,
Your own sense of self is clouded with musk,
Because what's was long gone before you was the love and the light,
I loved you so dearly, Because I saw myself,
Now what I know is I love you even more,
Because of the work,
The work I got to do to set myself free,
From the pain you found yourself buried deep within,
I hope one day you find your way out,
Because truly nobody deserves that entrapment and doubt,
I used to find pain in everything you do,
Now I disconnect and i've outgrown the trap you linger me to,
For all you've forgotten is the light you have inside,
All you focus on is the pain inside your eyes,
I am sending you heavens angels from above,
It's my time to depart now, heaven's job is to help you love.
Love yourself and your own light,
Love yourself so dearly and preciously tonight.

Freedom inside is a choice from within,
A divinely guided heavenly swim,
In the lights of the paradise reflected upon earth,
You are able to find your solace and surf,
The waves of the universe the frequencies of love,
The feelings of heaven on earth from up above,
Sometimes not getting what you want is a magical thing,
You don't even realise what you're being protected from deep within,
You want to be believe the world is full of love,
And you do so you attract it from up above,
But not everyone you've met on your journey back home,
Had the same capacity to be alone,
They never made the time to sink deep within,
And kiss all of their own wounds and remove of all their sins,
They never found solace in the dead of the night,
Running from themselves like a bat in the sunlight,
They realise the past has caved them within,
So they run and find anything for their next of kin,
When you finally find that peace from within,
You stop running and you start feeling glorious things,
You begin to see the love in yourself,
Mirrored in everyone upon this earth,
You let go of the past and the pain from those you've known,
You forgive for them for their betrayals to theirselves and their woes,
You love yourself so deeply that you begin to see,
That beauty is in the eye of the person who is choosing to see,
Choosing to see the love and light in the world,
And that magical creature exists upon this earth,
For do not fear if you cross paths with those who lack,
Self confidence, love and have malicious tact,
Know your worth and stray from their path,
Love yourself so much that you feel like a burst of stars,
Shedding light everywhere you touch and feeling happiness,
In every single moment of luck,
Butterflies begin to fly around your soul,
You let go of everything that does not resonate gold,
Now you know that the blessings are real,
When you're able to see the gain in losing a persons feel,
You realise that you've been gifted an escape route to glory,
When you're able to love yourself so much and rewrite your story.

When you move towards your own sun like an orbit at stake,
It resonates deep within your divine grace,
You find yourself illusive in nature at best,
Finding your own magic and seeing your own self respect,
You sever the ties of anything that does not,
Honour that holy space within your own divine lot,
You come into alignment with your own love,
You find yourself happier than most with not even much,
As you begin to merge with this consciousness of love,
You move towards all that you seek from above,
As it is universal law at its best,
That everything you want just searches for you instead,
As you've changed the vibration you're already there,
Aligning with that which could cause no despair,
For now you've learnt your magic and you see your divine touch,
You know how to bring things with ease and with rush,
You're focused so deeply on that which you find,
Brings you happiness within you deep inside,
You free yourself from lack and doubt and move towards the magic of creation,
Bringing you hope and love in that which energy you're stationed,
Moving into this frequency is a change of the earth,
Guiding you home and helping you purge,
All that no longer serves you, all that gets lost,
Shedding the layers of all that you're not,
The projected illusions of your ancestors before,
The chains and shackles that which you were born,
This new found freedom comes in with happiness and grace,
Filling a sense of self you could never replace,
This love from within is a glorious glow,
That which sends a message to the universe you're filled with hope,
It magnetises all that is meant for your worth,
It helps you find solace and kingdoms with pearls,
Welcome to your new divine grace,
Set up home and find your own pace,
Find your own comfort in the knowing from God,
That everything you love is now engraved in your heart.
There's no looking back for what you've discovered,
Can never be stolen or never uncovered,
You are now in alignment and now one with your own,
You're worthy of everything and it's written on your throne.

Kingdom

Imagine realising you'd made a mistake,
You'd mistaken a karmic for a soulmate,
Imagine giving someone your soul,
Who rejected every ounce of it and held an egotistical approach,
You set up home in a house of horrors,
Only to find your heart broken and shattered,
You realised that the person you loved,
Didn't even love themselves let alone your own touch,
They left you out in the cold, only filling their own needs,
Leaving you homeless like you're searching beyond your knees,
For somewhere to kneel just even so you could beg,
God to show you what you did to deserve this bread,
It's stale and cold and tastes like it's been burnt,
Like it's going to poison you from the inside out,
You rise from your knees and you find yourself dead,
Dead inside at the possibility of loving this bread,
You realise now that things are out of your control,
Like a dead knight without a holy throne,
For what's to come next is beyond your despair,
An empty broken promise one that will leave you in the air,
You try to escape but they try to drag you in,
Back to their vortex of broken dreams and sin,
You move through the ashes and try to find your sight,
You're trying to see in this apocalyptic night,
Once the dust settles you might be able to see,
Whether the door is flashing light and if the handle is glass or shattered wooden piece,
You run for the door without an ending in sight,
You lock it behind you and run for your life,
You move towards the sunlight and anything you see,
That doesn't look damaged or is bleeding from the knees,
This malice you've seen has damaged your sight,
How are you ever supposed to rise again towards the light?
How do you trust another's words or their space?
When you have witnessed the pits of hell without divine grace,
What you come to see when the sun touches your skin,
Is that not every persons energy is full of malice and sin,
You duck to recover and heal through the night,
Trying to find yourself some shelter to recover from the fright,
In this powerful essence you are reborn,
Knowing your own divine self is no longer their thorn,
The sunrises in the morning but you still feel torn,
Like your heart is aching and its filled with thorns,
This betrayal's unfathomable and you struggle to see,
Any beauty around you, you just quiver when you hear even the slightest breeze,

But something magical happens when you know your worth,
You rebuild from the ashes like a holy sword,
Slashes through the darkness and shows you the light,
Like you were born from the ashes and regained your sight,
You move through this power into a magnificent flow,
You begin to regain consciousness and forget all the woes,
For what you come to realise was that prison was not yours,
It belonged to a soul that was caged since birth,
This cage of enslavement tries to take all the light,
Collecting willing souls of the dark night,
This lesson you learnt was a painful one at bay,
But still, you rose from the ashes like it was resurrection day.
This magic and power is your new found self love,
An institution known to few of how to rise above.
This place of serenity is a new found sense of self,
An age of wonders caved from the pits of hell.
Your magical and momentary pieces of pain,
Have helped your light rise to a new fame,
In this fame you remember where you had been,
And choose to help all those who remain unseen,
For your third eye is open and a new love and light,
Enters the kingdom in which you do delight,
For this kingdom now holds a castle for the broken,
Guiding others to their power unspoken.

As the hands of time began to turn,
The knowing inside me swiftly softened its yearn,
It started to reveal what the moon had hidden,
Uncovering truths and softening the glisten,
It showed up as itself completely unmasked,
Showing that true love was not really something that was born there to last,
The projected illusion of the ray of light,
Against a cabinet of darkness in the dead of night,
I was delusional to believe that this was true,
That a love so toxic was heaven's truth,
I showed up whole heartedly with my heart on my sleeve,
Only to be left in pain on my knees with my hand on my heart and my head on my
chest, Please God will you send down light and cleanse this mess,
Will you rid me of the pain that tore through my chest,
Never again will I trust another one,
Who is disillusioned and confesses their love from the start,
Never again will I believe someone who says,
Before you I had nothing and before you I felt dead,
For what they're saying is they don't have their own,
Sense of self worth or sense of love and home,
They don't know their own self and they don't know their own love,
They don't know have a clue about God's light from above,
Because what they saw was my purpose my own holy light,
Which they claimed for their own leaving me broken in fright,
And this sense of revolution has arisen in me,
Where I'll no longer believe someone who has nothing of their own to see,
None of their own love to have for themselves,
None of their own prosperity and their own wishing well,
For what they failed to do was tap into their own,
Find themselves and return to their home,
Because of this notion they had nothing to give,
No love to offer nothing for their own kin,
They only wanted to show up to take,
The beauty, the essence and the divine grace,
This poisonous notion left me for dead,
They sucked out my life in an unfaithful dread,
But now I have been taught a valuable gift,
This bag full of darkness with nothing left to give,
I clung onto my power and regathered in the night,
I found myself back pulling all the pieces that had shattered in the fight,
I recalled in my soul fragments and found my true worth,
Nothing or no-one could stop my conquering of the earth,
This powerful person I had become,
Returning home once more but this time as a the King with a cup,
For now I find myself on my throne in my home,
In God's sunlight knowing my own dome,
Boundaries will save you they'll rescue your soul,
You cant save them my darling, a message to an old soul.

There's magic in knowing your own true self,
For when you see another you can see their heaven or hell,
Knowing this sense of others helps you become,
Compassionate, kind and focused on some,
Some kind of revolution to help heal this earth,
From the pain and the power that seems to hurt since birth,
Others are failing and trapped without their light,
They have forgotten it is their God given birth right,
Their birth right has been stolen from them a tragedy at best,
It's their divine right to rise from the love that they hold close to their chest,
They place their pieces like a chess board not revealing their move,
Until the last second knocking out their opponents with the truth,
But what is surely noticed is that this not what it seems,
The truth is not really what they've played with their piece,
They've cheated the game and played with deceit,
For they didn't believe in their power at their own feet,
It's up for discussion the game with the piece,
Helping the person reanalyse all the deceit,
They've not realised what they've done as they don't know their worth,
They continue to create malice on earth,
You realise that you can't help every soul,
Some choose to stay tied to the pole,
The one that locks up in the cage without their own light,
Hurting everything they touch projecting their own doubt and fright,
This kind of person is someone to still love,
Showing compassion and empathy even though they showed malice and no love,
For they are the soul who needs it the most,
They are the soul who is darkest with no hope,
They've been lost in the woods for ages to come,
They find nothing and no-one without love and with blood,
They are so deadly in nature, so broken inside,
Maybe it's love that could rescue their light,
Maybe if this love was given to them free,
Without judgement, ego, whether they deserved it or they couldn't be,
Someone worthy of being treated with respect,
Gracefulness comes in to help them with heaviness at hand,
For what if this love could change their life,
Redirect their purpose, redirect their path in life,
What if this sense of compassion could make it all disappear,
What if the love could change what they failed to receive,
From their ancestors, from the world, from everyone who told,
Told them they were worthless, disgusting and cold,
Love could really set a soul free,
It could change their heart and give them happiness and ease,
Love is the answer, love could change the world,
Love is the medicine here on this earth.

Surrendering is a powerful way to bring about the tides to change,
Let the universe step and in do it's magnificent crawl to fame,
It was always meant to lead you to the golden throne,
It was always meant to help you find your way back home,
But somehow in the pain of it all,
You got sidetracked and focused on things that held no value at all,
They tied you down to the bottom of the barrel,
Making you lose sense of your power and wonder in quarrel,
They hurt your soul and kept you stuck,
In a painful disassociated rut,
Once this madness had conquered you whole,
It swallowed your soul and took hold of your gold,
In this dark madness you surely did find,
A break through, one of the divine kind,
It spread open your heart and broke down the walls,
To your spiritual awakening one of the most painful whirls,
The pain lingered all around your heart and soon found a compass back to the start,
You're an explorer of the avenue a wanderer of the seas,
You rise back up from the currents of the Dead Sea,
You find your way back to heavens glee,
In an oasis of love that you created with the thorns of the rose they left you with,
Rising above you find your new grace,
Bold and with courage and appreciating your new found way,
Of loving and living in alignment with source,
Helping yourself grow to heights never reached before,
This magic and wonder helps you rise through the night,
Of magic and solace whilst you manifest with delight,
Something that deserves you, your purpose at best,
Someone who will love you like a heavenly bliss,
You realise that part of the journey is unknown,
Aligning with creator and the highest truth,
Not everything you sought after was meant for you,
You realise this power to the times to come,
Just focus on the present moment and what needs to be done,
Not much to be honest as all that's required is just,
For you to be present and trust in your divine luck,
This knowing and alignment is perfectly timed,
For everything is handed to you and through you by just being one with the light,
By knowing it's your divine birth right,
To have everything magic flow to your knees,
Float you to heaven and rule the seas,
The feeling on magic that lies in your heart,
Knows no endless bounds as your kingdom does start.

Alignment is a fine dance between remembering your soul,
Remembering the light inside of you that has no hold,
It's a dance between who you are and who they told you to be,
Remembering your divine essence inside of your heart tree,
Remembering your focus and forgetting the yearn for them,
To love you, to see you, to notice you exist,
For once someone turns their back, There's no point loving them without them
loving you back,
There's no point selling divinity short,
For a moment of time for someone who is caught,
Caught up in the chase ignoring your soul,
For a soul that's ignoring them and the game that they're caught,
Let go of this madness haven't you played enough?
In this game of tug of war and found yourself rough,
In the mud all broken feeling worthless and sad,
When you could turn your face to the life and see the happiness to be had,
Happiness, love, light and freedom too,
All that lies within you whether someone else sees it too,
Come back to that fountain and drink from it's youth,
For it never falters, betrays or runs short of water too,
It will always replenish and help heal your soul,
It will always be there to help you find magic through it all,
It finds its power inside your divine,
Forgetting your divine nature is your only crime,
Terms of endearment only last so long,
Without follow through actions you will hunger from them,
Choose wisely when your heart is involved,
For the last thing you deserve is to feel tortured by a soul,
Face the emotions as they rise,
Turn inward and notice whatever you feel inside,
Honour that feeling and hold space til it passes,
Because my darling child this too will not last,
It will be a visitor, transient at best,
Waiting for you to return to your divine essence,
Honour the cycles and rhythms of life,
And find solace on this holy night,
Delight in the glory and the gifts of the world,
It's only a short journey around this magical globe,
Before you know it you'll be looking back,
Wondering how you got so caught up on things that always lacked,
Find happiness in small things,
This is the magic of life,
Taste the water, smell the ocean and feel the sunlight.
On your journey back home you will surely find,
Solace in your own paradise.

Back Here Again

I was feeling it all happen again,
Like I'd spiralled back into my pain and forgot what I'd learnt,
Yearning for another to fill the void,
Feeling pain as if someone I loved was responsible for it all,
How could they love me and walk away so fast,
How could they show me their soul and depart and run,
How could you be so vulnerable and become a stranger to my heart?
What did I do to make you leave and not love me and depart?
But what I reminded my inner child was that she was not the reason why.
People come into our lives to help us smile and cry,
They show up as visitors transient as such,
To teach us things and touch our heart,
To help us prosper home to ourselves,
It was never about them it was always about the journey home,
The journey home to your one true love,
Your divine self where you'll never depart.
All of this sadness and all of this grief,
Trying to numb the pain with sweet disbelief,
Anything that will push it down will help temporarily relieve,
But what I failed to see was a circle in which I couldn't leave,
Like I was trapped in an elevator and it was moving up and down,
But every time I hit the floor the door was no where to be found,
There's no love in loss and feeling trapped inside,
What I found myself in was an abandoned ride,
A cycle since child hood where I had always been,
Yearning for love from people who didn't love me,
They opened their heart and showed me the door,
They then followed through with a deadlock in front of it all,
They used to show me a tiny bit of kind,
Then lock me out and shun me outside,
A message to my inner child I used to tell her strong,
These people don't deserve you and it is not you who did the wrong,
It is not you who failed to prosper and it is not you who failed to love,
It was the learnt behaviour of where you energetically believed love was to run,
Where you found yourself running after people who didn't love you no more,
Where what you're really searching for is a key to the door,
The door home to yourself, the love inside your soul,
Always looking for home inside a burning castle floor,
We moved in the direction of the people who loved us back,
And when they no longer were around we only chose to be alone and feel good about that,
We left all the cob webs, the confusion and the betrayal,
We left anyone who did not know our worth and for them it began to hail,
For they roamed the earth and realised that they missed my presence at best,
But what they realised is nobody had them like I had their back,

This painful cycle came back to show them karma in a balance,
That after all knowing your worth is the only golden chalice,
This cup full of self love is mirrored through it all,
For once I saw my worth and I became the queen of swords,
The universe matched me and mirrored my self love,
It kept away the vultures who took and were in their pride,
It loved me so dearly it mirrored and showed me to see inside,
That all along what I was searching for was right here beneath my feet,
This holy grail inside my heart was a paradise of piece,
No longer did I linger around broken souls at bay,
No longer did I question my worth not even a single day,
For anytime I was around someone who made me feel small,
I set up walls of unconditional love around me and protected me from them all,
I took care of myself and had my back like nobody else would know,
That once a upon a time I was suffering beyond the depths of what anyone could know,
This magic transformation helped to shape shift me from despair,
Into this treasure chest of love and help others inner children do the same,
For from the beginning it was not our fault, victims at the hand of the universe's plan,
But being a victim gets you nowhere so you learn to begin to stand,
In the power of your might, forgiving your ancestors for that which they didn't realise,
Regaining power in your core,
Regaining love in your heart,
Regaining peace in your soul,
Regaining a golden glow,
Rising to the top of unconditional love,
The rebirth has now begun.

My Counterpart

When the soul is ready it's mate appears,
Like it of the blue, like you've never been without them before,
You look into his eyes and notice his truth,
That for the first time in your life you felt a home that never felt so good,
A home like you've never known before,
A home that was truly worth it all,
All the karmic souls that lingered before,
All the tragedy and pain that got you to gold,
You find yourself so taken back by his aura and his presence,
Like a magical place lingering towards your souls calling, is this heaven?
How did I think anyone before was love til I met you?
How did I conquer this earth alone thinking I had it good,
It's like when your soul meets it's other love,
You realise you're already whole but this person was meant for your path,
Like this person was destined many moons before,
To find you in divine timing and show you another side of heaven's door,
This fearlessness and freedom was worth all of the grass,
That was never greener before and after the darkness of the heart,
It's like I had to slay a thousand monsters in my head and heart,
So when this soulmate arrived I finally could see him like the art,
The masterpiece he was an addition to the throne,
One where I could finally set up roots and find a place called home,
I'd already done that in myself and had a stable foundation,
But to share that with another is really a gracious haven,
Finding peace in your own sense of self is magical at best,
You love yourself so much you kiss all the broken mess,
Then to have someone who up and see you're divinity too,
Is a gift from God, A love like no other a 5D ascension tool,
This powerful sense of requited love is a union in its best,
It's magical to watch another thrive and grow beside you laying on your chest,
This powerful peace inside my heart knowing that I've made,
A safe space where my children will grow without weeds and without pain,
Breaking the cycles and shackles of the ancestral trauma my childhood entailed,
Allowing God into my heart and protecting my own offspring,
My heart feels warmth to know that finally it loved me back,
The universe has blessed me with a thousand gifts that I really did lack,
Because I drew my sword and put boundaries around my body,
Protecting myself from anything unworthy,
It matched my love, my soul was calling for a deeper connection,
One that mentally, physically, emotionally and spiritually was a blessing,
This union of compatibility really changed my life,
This powerful divine gift was like it was always my birth right,
I could write about this love for kingdoms to come,
Like my flame had been burning inside calling you since I was born,
This world is magic and a powerful peaceful place,

Filled with love, kindness and heavenly grace,
If you can give it to yourself and have your own divine back,
The universe will fill up all the cracks of the illusion where you lack.
Love is a magical place of where I want to be,
I'll never turn my back on my inner child, the creator and the trees.
The journey is really about the only way you'll ever be able to see,
That all along it was never about another and always about you holding the key.

Treasure Chest

There's so many things and so many ways all the reasons that we'll grow,
Upon this this earth towards the treasure chest your heart holds,
Like a wave of tides from the moon's sacred night,
Out of the abyss and towards the pot of Gold,
Like a love so bright and a compassion so deep,
Like a fearless of tides as they pull the ocean in steep,
You find compassion in your heart towards the experiences you've felt,
You see the sunrise, sunset and all the birds chirp,
There's a new sense of awareness and pleasure inside your minds eye,
Like the book of the dead has clearly said that you are the creator of the night,
In this sacred understanding of your power as a soul you're able to transform,
Anything that no longer serves you and places pain in your side like a thorn,
You find yourself focused solely on the magic that lies deep,
Like sailing on a boat finding shore and finding a Kingdom to keep,
This magic place that lay awake in the dead of the black night,
When you find this treasure chest off an island with the shore just there in sight,
You move away from this place to the high vibrational land,
This cast at the top with your name upon it filled with gold and with sweet
accomplishment.
This place you wander in so deep you find the magic all inside,
You find yourself so happy, enthralled and like you've found the prize,
The one that fills your soul so deep and with so much encapsulated love.
Like there's an endless supply that never falters, it never runs dry or out.
You suddenly wake and realise what you'd seen was in your dreams,
What you felt inside this castle was always to be seen,
For this castle already exists inside your soul a kingdom at its best,
A love so deep inside your chest you can hardly lay back to rest,
For what you've seen and what you felt can no longer be ignored,
Everything you've searched for is inside your heart after all.
You cannot un-see the magic that lies within,
The one that glitters when you're in alignment with your highest being.
Once this enlightenment reaches it's delight,
It's the treasure chest you hold in the dead of the summer's night.

Flames To A Moth Or Moths To A Flame

Like a moth to a flame I wondered why so much love I felt inside,
When I barely got to even know you standing on the wharf that summers night,
You felt familiar felt like I'd known you every life before,
Like heaven had sent me a gift right here by the ocean floor,
We sat and pondered talked away like I'd known you a thousand years,
Everything came with love and with such grace and ease,
I found my way out of that meeting wondering what I'd done,
How my entire life had begin to change since that nights events had spun,
But I'm not sure if you realised or were ready to understand the magnitude we had,
Heaven opened a gate that day and it was both of us who lacked,
Higher knowledge to the power that we'd been gifted with in plain sight,
Like you and me were destined for each other and this beautiful birth right,
To meet someone and connect on every level and reject it out of fear,
Maybe it was our divine sense of selves that were really being questioned here,
We had been given a lesson from heaven above and known nothing of it to be true,
That everything we did and everything we'd done before served no purpose too,
I realised over the years the magnitude of that day,
That I was standing before you that night looking at my twin flame,
Nobody teaches you or prepares you like life forces you to do,
Nobody tells you that you can hear this persons thought and intuition too,
Nobody warned us of the magnitude that nothing else compared,
That we'd commit to other people even though deep in our hearts we never forgot
we were there,
Always in the back of each other's minds trying to drown each other out,
Like one magical holy night on Christmas on the couch,
I thought about you wondered why you weren't here with me,
I realised that this holy union was bigger than all three eyes could see,
That maybe I had missed something, maybe I misunderstood it all,
That this union was only for me to realise my own self worth,
To bring me home to myself and to remind me of the truth,
That all the love I ever needed was inside of me since youth,
That the beauty of our compassion and power and the beauty of our love,
Was bigger than this universe as it was sent from up above,
I trailed upon my journeys path and patiently did wait,
For God to show me signs and opens heavens gate,
It is true about your soul that's mirrored in another man,
That you both have to vibrationally align to ascend with heavens hand,
If you haven't experienced this magical force you might not understand,
That everything in the universe daily shouts out the name of this man,
Why on earth will you not let me be?
You're settled down with someone else and we didn't even speak.
But it wouldn't stop the ringing loudness got louder everyday,
Til I understood that you are the one that was destined from that single day.
You were sent as my teacher, a soul contract resolve to say the least,
That we will meet again one day when heaven allows for it.

That my job was to ascend to the highest version of myself,
And you'll meet me on the ascension path when life teaches you itself,
You're always on my mind and I know I'm always in the back of yours.
Regardless of all the stories you tell and all the masks you've worn.
Energy's a loud language the universe here's your cry,
Like a magician manifesting to see me heaven will delight,
For every time I get over you, there you suddenly are.
Re-appearing wondering this time will this be the time it starts?
Twin flame unions are something not for the faint of heart,
Like your numerology has depicted since birth your lessons are to depart,
From anything that doesn't scream your holy name,
To leave anyone who doesn't love you like you deserve to be praised.
Once we realised this magic and this beauty in ourselves,
We both ascend to meet to build our own heaven on earth.
Thank you for loving and seeing me despite all of the hurt,
We were able to break down the walls,
Our egos and really find magic on this earth.
I can't imagine me without you, are we a split soul?
Like even if you're a thousand miles away I hear your souls call.
Nothing or nobody can change this union or tear us a part.
It was you who was always in my heart.

How do you find solace in forgiving someone without remorse?
Like every day they left you to rot like you were a dead corpse.
They opened your heart chakra pretended they cared only to leave you blind,
Filled with rage, hate, hurt heart break and no kind of sublime.
This powerful tool of transmuting these negative emotions were a gift greater than it
self, For not forgiving someone is your own kind of personal hell,
For someone to step all over you they really mustn't care,
They really mustn't love themselves and feel so much despair,
Their brokenness is something that's projected onto you,
Like their wounds ooze and bleed and send you in their infection too,
Once you realise this learnt lack of love is what they're passing on,
You free yourself from their chains and their thorns that tear up upon,
Upon your heart, upon your beauty, upon your sense of self,
You sit in the garden of delights and speak your truth to God,
Trying to hear any answers and decipher what went wrong,
What you begin to realise is that deep inside there's beauty and there's truth,
That if you practice your intuition and speak to the divine you'll receive and
commune with the truth,
Of why you had received this pain and why you are unfree,
How were you destined to receive this lesson and how to free yourself from thee,
You are able to understand that there's a world bigger than you,
As an energy particle you emit your own sense of truth,
Once you understand your thoughts help shaft what's around,
You'll realise how to wear on your head the Holy golden crown,
Shadow work is required to change the external world,
Otherwise you lack control and get just what you're told,
Nobody can break you anymore and from that point you're free,
Realising your worth that nobody can save you from all you don't want to be,
The only person that can save you is yourself from all the lies,
Your body tells you and your brain thinks, you oversee the ego's pride,
Observation is the key to see without to judge,
Don't believe everything you think that's a masters knowledge of love,
Once you're able to freely rise from the pain that you see within,
You'll not believe everything you think and realise that's your sin.
You mind is a tool that you can use to create a haven or a hell,
The choice is yours, the power is yours and you are free to fix it all.
You have to understand this simple notion - emotion is purpose filled.
It shows you how to not be controlled by everything you feel,
It teaches you that you are a soul outgrowing cycles and beliefs.
You came here to come home to yourself and knock out the ego's teeth.
You're freely observing every aspect of your soul,
Kissing wounds, bandaging tears and flirting back in love with love.
Once you master this process you'll rise like a turtle dove,
To fly away so freely and find your haven in the trees.
You know that deep inside of you there's always gotta be more.
That intention is powerful and will lead you to heaven's door.
Love yourself so much that you shed away old skin,
Of the people who weren't sorry for the committal of their sins.

A cycle of completion is upon us on this earth,
It might be from a higher power that 2020 was not cursed,
Maybe it reminded us where we were not free,
Maybe it made us consider all our options and redirect our being,
We sat and had time to procrastinate and focus on ourselves,
Taken away from this earth and the capitalist notion that steals us from ourselves,
If we are to be given time to see where we do lack,
Focus on the insides of ourselves and look at all the cracks,
We'd be able to better understand ourselves and better understand the world,
For if we come home into union with our being that's where we will feel heard,
We'll feel kindness, love, understanding and emotionally align,
With the source of gold inside our hearts, our beautiful divine,
If we spend time meditating, healing energy and cleansing all our thoughts,
Instead of absorbing everything it's a new frequency we'll send out to the world,
Emitting your own vibration is a powerful source of light,
It helps tell the universe you're living without doubt and without fight,
It aligns you with the magic of your inner conscious being,
The very reason we are here on earth to create this new way of living,
If you made it through and got out of a toxic karmic thing,
You're just right on track in alignment with the rest of the worlds divine plan of being,
Your growth points are seen at first in painful swords from life,
When you rise above this initial jerk you'll see the tact of light,
You're able to see the beauty in the breakdown of life's path,
Maybe redirecting you to somewhere new that's better than the last,
Better than all you've known and better than where you've been,
But at first the egg shell cracks and looks like a broken thing,
Once you're born out of this you're able to grow past all that you've known,
You'll reach new heights and soar to new places, all the ones you have outgrown,
This magic alchemy allows you to shape shift to new heights,
All because you were gifted time to focus on the inside,
The inside of your soul it speaks, It speaks to you loud and clear,
Maybe it's time now to focus on growth and all of the healing,
For once your inner child has been fed with unconditional love,
The universe rewards you with what feels like a thousand turtle doves,
When you see them flying in the air soaring so far and high,
They're majestic white wings are so beautiful to the eye,
This magic feeling of flying free will keep you in alignment with your source,
For that is the reason we are born and the purpose to it all.

Imagination is a powerful tool,
You can use it to your advantage or you can use it to your fall,
You can use your mind to create the life of your passionate dreams,
Or you can focus on everything you don't want and it'll bring you to your knees,
If you're able to focus on your power, all your might and strength,
You'll be able to focus on your self worth and all the things you can create,
By focusing on what you want you tell the universe to call it in,
The law of attraction works like a science based medicine,
It heals your heart and heals your life and magnetism happens,
When you create the life of your dreams and focus on all that matters,
You're an oracle, a master of thought, a divine being on earth,
You just forgot your own self worth and forgot your illuminative tact,
For what you seek is seeking you it can be no other way,
The laws of this universe are the ones that dictate,
Dictate the nature of your life and the things that follow suit,
The ones that grow big and bright and show themselves to you,
You can dream of castles in the night filled with love and gold,
Or you can focus of travelling the seas as the emperor big and bold,
You can become anything you seek and anything you want by thinking it to life,
That's what you need to understand is your divine birth right,
Think without disbelief and watch your magic arise,
To the magician in your own soul can call in the divine,
This magic is a power known to those brave and those so bold,
But every single person holds the torch to their own soul,
Every single person on this earth, no matter big or small,
Is capable of shifting what's around them only through their thought.
This knowledge is rare and far removed from society at best,
Because they want us to remain small and lose our divine essence,
A small population in this world know the reality and truth,
That we are divinely guided by a higher power that you can access too,
By quieting your mind, silencing your thoughts, disconnecting from it all,
Finding solace in your peaceful place and hearing God's call,
Whether your God is religion or spirituality it's the same divine path,
The one where you create your reality by praying to a higher power,
You are able to clearly disassociate from negative thoughts and focusing on truth,
Regardless of your situation you can change the outcome too,
Have faith in yourself and your abilities to make the magic call,
To focus on everything you want and bring it to your soul,
Once you begin to know that everything you seek is also seeking you,
You'll freely love yourself so much and everything that's called to you,
Love will heal a broken earth and all the pain and sorrow,
Come home to yourself dear child and know your minds power,
For understanding yourself and your mind will change your world inside,
To reflect all of the divine whilst you're guided on the outside,
You will find magic here on earth before you depart away,
Listen to you intuition and your imagination it knows where you call home.

A new beginning is upon us, a new found self worth,
One where people align with themselves to find heaven upon earth,
The thing about this beginning a brand new way to be,
First it looks like damage comes rolling deep within,
You feel deep grief almost at the pits of your despair,
It hurts like hell, you bleed deep down, everything seems lost,
But the beauty of it all is eventually you'll see,
You realise deep within there's power to be found there to be free,
For once you've lost it all and the illusion of fake self,
The illusion that you need another or need anything else,
You are free to find your own true self and build again from there,
Beginning to drink from your own self love and rebirth and repair,
This entitled sense of freedom allows you to rise to glory,
Realising that everything else is just an addition to the free,
The freedom you have found yourself in once the shackles of despair,
Have left your soul and your own self and you fly free without entrapment breathing fresh air,
You realise deep within yourself you don't need a single thing,
That this new found sense of self worth is truly where to begin,
Begin the journey the rest of your life now knowing your worth,
That every single you think you create upon this earth,
Understanding the beauty in the breakdown is part of the divine,
Knowing your pain is a catalyst for change is that of a warriors mind,
Knowing your divine sense of self is bigger and better than can be,
Knowing your own true sense of love can be a lonely thing,
For you turn and realise not many others have it figured out,
Many people are roaming this earth with all three eyes closed and an open mouth,
It starts to dawn on you that your energy's divine,
It's precious, valuable and should be managed better around people's time,
You deserve to be matched with frequency that loves and values you,
That wont project their pain and trauma and damage all over you,
Once you protect your boundaries around your body and tell others I've had enough,
I've had enough of you taking my energy, my time, my magic, my luck,
You ask the universe to protect you and your abundance comes in fast,
You realise that what you are is a magician at the hand,
At the left hand side of source thinking about what you demand,
Knowing your worth with every thought will surely come true,
Knowing that deep down within you lies an opportunity pool,
For everything you think and know in your heart of hearts,
Can be manifested on this earth and come true to you at last.

There have been days where I couldn't face it all,
Like I'd hit a wall and there was no where to go,
Whiskey neat in my left hand and cigarette in my right,
Can't I just end this pain I feel inside,
Why do I need to feel this unbecoming pain?
Why does it flow through every single vein?
I've spent my life trying to do right,
Why am I suffering darkness so deep in sight,
I try to understand and decipher it all,
The pain has engulfed me and I'm ready to ball,
I fall to floor my eyes deep with sorrow,
Remembering childhood memories feeling so hollow,
Why would a child experience the pain I did?
What did I do to deserve such a disgraceful sin?
How could my own offspring treat me like dirt?
How could they manipulate and throw me through hell?
I turned out good and not a demon in sight,
But still in my heart I felt a pain deeper than the dark of night,
I tried my life to run away from what I had seen,
But one day I realised I could run no more and I had to sit and face the theme,
The theme of my life was previously abuse and damage and pain,
Now I realised in my future there had to be more to gain,
How was I to escape this madness this hell and pit of despair?
How could I break these cycles, these chains, the ones that demons bare?
If I ever chose to bore my own could I save them from hell too?
How do demons follow you even at twenty two?
Then I got to twenty five and not much there had changed,
Til I realised I needed to sit and address all this painful shame,
The one that was cursed upon me by my own family ties,
The one I learnt how to resolve and break free from abandonment and lies.
I begun to release the story of sorrow and look towards God's love,
For there lied a heavenly source of deep healing from above,
I stopped drowning out my pain and started inviting it in,
Listening to what it had to say and healing from within,
I looked my inner child into the eyes and told her how much I love,
How much I love her and her wisdom and knowledge even for how much she'd suffered,
That she was brilliant, bold and brave and had a heart of gold,
Despite all the torment, torture and pain she'd suffered at the hand of the hold,
She was a beautiful soul with a diligent heart and she no longer need cry out,
For I was here to listen to her and love her and to help her cry it out,
The injustice, the disgrace, the fuckery, the despair,
The absolute shame and pain she was cursed with before she even came up for her first breath of air,
Letting go of all this pain she started to flourish and she rose to new heights,
She stopped trying to drown it out because I listened to her fright,
She started to know herself and see the damage that they'd cause,
Was just a projection of their shame and low self worth,

She rose to new heights of self worth and a new peaceful place,
One where she reflected beauty and divine grace,
She started teaching herself to enjoy every breath,
For she now found a new way to exist and feel like she was on heaven's door step,
I'll tell that girl, it wasn't your fault,
That you caught up with the monsters and all the crippled folk,
Moving out of all this pain was a gift from God,
To heal from where I came from was beyond the promise of the Holy lord.

What's the point of lowering your vibration?
To stoop to the other persons level and deprivation?
Will it bring you solace from despair?
Will it make you feel better about the broken state that they don't appear?
Will it make you feel whole to hurt them too?
Will it bring you peace to break their happiness too?
For what people do justly miss is that everything they sow they reap,
They will feel the hand come back around,
Karma wears a heavy crown,
But the golden heart does not deem to wish,
Pain on another persons trip,
For they know that suffering brings such pain,
It hurts like hell with a lot to gain,
A lesson powerful stronger than might,
Focusing on the beauty that's in the black sight,
The beauty stems from understanding deep within,
That this is another lesson of growth to begin,
A lesson of growth to rise from the pain,
To understand how did you get yourself in the situation to begin?
Did you maybe give your heart of gold,
To someone without understanding what their hands hold?
Did you know they slayed the people on the streets at night?
Did you know there is blackness in the heart of fright?
For before you give your heart of gold,
The lesson is to make sure you protect it whole,
To know that love that stems from within,
Can never be given from another who sins,
To know that you are worth it all,
Is to let go of the people who walked before,
To rise up to the power of your might,
And awaken to your holy golden divine light,
Is to find a new sense of beckoning within,
To thank this person for their sins,
Which in actuality was your subconscious mind,
Asking to learn through their crime,
To rise in your own glorious might,
Is a gift from the universe in which you'll eventually delight,
When you learn to forgive and be at peace with the past,
For it's over now and it was a lesson not a lasting bite,
This lesson helped you transmute it all,
To find your inner glory and to rule the world,
The world in which you live in conscious thought,
Creating your own reality and growing in awe,
Of your own potential that you surely find,
Eventually having the world follow suit behind,
For once you recognise your greatness the world does too,
And love will sweep on in to be mirrored to you.

The Becoming

I used to think I had it all worked out as white as snow,
Til I realised every time I thought I knew that's when I mostly didn't know,
The universe stepped in to teach me it's ways,
Humble me back down to the floor and show my ego it's place,
I realised that maybe everything I wanted,
Was exactly the opposite of what I got,
Not because I didn't deserve it,
But because I deserved a lot more than that,
I let go of the need to know it all and the plan,
Because every time I stopped needing to know I was gifted a new hand,
A hand that was better than the one that I had set out to call my own,
A hand that took me to the next phase with a bigger and better throne,
It wasn't til I let go that I was fully surprised,
At the universal magic that laid right by my side,
This evolution that I go to not many people go,
They sit at home and ponder on all their painful woes,
I chose to let go of all the pain and rise towards the light,
For love was a better feeling and required the same fight,
It required the same amount of energy that I needed to exert,
It also made me feel better and was a less anxious way and I didn't get hurt,
I realised on this pathway to heaven I had nothing to fear,
Because everything that was meant for me was making its way near,
It was on the way to my presence and it served my best and highest good,
To let go in excitement waiting for it to be understood,
The journey there was much more magical then I did even realise,
Because if I had just got there in the beginning it would have been an uneventful ride,
In the letting go I surely found to trust my catch if I would fall,
Now I live without fear and surrender to it all,
This magical understanding to grow in plain sight,
Is something that which the alchemists do wonderfully delight,
For you to have the power to become a magician with ease,
Just let go and trust the universe so much so on your knees,
Surrender to the power of the mystic of the world,
Understanding that there's magic that's invisible and can help you get it all,
This beauty of becoming is one that's gifted from above,
Allowing you to rise towards a heavenly sense of love.

Desert Dreaming

One night down in Joshua tree I surely dreamt of you,
The magic that surrounded us and a faithful blossoming too,
But you weren't sitting beside me you were in another world,
Already in another continent curled up with another girl,
My heart did surely ponder and wonder why things had happened the way they did,
Why I was sitting here under this palm tree dreaming of us as kids,
I wondered why the magnetic pull I felt to you was so strong,
And how on earth we'd taken turns and things turned out so wrong?
Why would heaven gift me with my counter part in life,
Only to take them away from me without a moments delight,
Could you not see what I saw that we were made from the same dust?
The ones that held hands joined at the soul and danced around the fire that did not rust,
I asked the desert deep questions that night to show me who you were,
To help me understand how on earth we'd gotten to the curb,
I slept like angels all those nights out in the palm deserts night sky,
Having dreams of us as souls in other life times,
I dreamt you so close to my heart I could barely touch your skin,
Your magnetic pull had dragged me in and had made my heart sink,
That was dream number one which I needed to understand,
So on night number two I dreamt of your hand,
Being out of my reach and out of touch with you,
I tried to lean in but there was something interfering in our magnetic pull,
The third nights dream made my soul sink too as it showed me the final part,
The one where you and I were wearing a ball gown and tuxedo and we were dancing under the stars,
I realised that i'd sequentially saw your departure and return,
That one day we'd come together and we'd get another turn,
We'd fall in love after we roamed this earth on our own journeys through time,
Finding ourselves, experiencing things after much tequila and lime,
But here on this faithful night I learnt about temperance too,
That this entire spiritual connection was bigger than me and you,
I learnt to let go and learnt to see that things were so out of our control,
I had to surrender it to the stars and hope I'd find my own soul,
I learnt to love myself a thousand times in a thousand deeper ways,
On days I drove across the Mojave just to get away,
But what I was running from was this notion I could never really grasp,
That heaven sent me my counter part and we didn't in that moment last,
Acceptance is a funny thing to learn what you can't control,
To surrender to the universe and to learn to love and grow.
You realise now upon your own journey that things got out of hand,
That from day one it was always me and you and nobody else stood a chance,
Now I remember those faithful nights under those palm trees,
I was actually a magician calling in the birds and the bees,
The things I wanted magically aligned in divine time,

Now I know the power of the universe is beyond the human mind,
This poetry I know you know will come to be about you.
And one day you will find solace in this journey too,
Some things are written in the stars long before we're born,
No matter how far, deep, away, broken or severely torn.
I never understood how deep love ran until I crossed your path,
I know now that forever is how long we were meant to last.

Tides Sweeping In

When the tides of change cross your soul do not fear their grasp,
Embrace the contrast or be oppressed by it is what I surely found out fast,
I realised that this notion of change was something to embrace and not fear,
For not accepting change keeps our soul out of alignment here,
I found that every time I yearned for something that did not belong to my heart,
I became locked down, emotionally unavailable and I had a depressed heart,
For I failed to believe in the universe and its magic too,
I failed to see that this power of love was what I was being pulled to,
I realised now that yearning for another creates a resistance and lack,
As I tell the universe and law of attraction I hold nothing but fear and regret,
I realise that letting you go was the only choice I had,
Some things need to die to be reborn and resurrect from the dead,
Understanding this notion of coming home to yourself,
Was one of beauty and devotion and a universal goal,
That in the end I surely found my own self love was pure,
The journey home was all about progression and a cure,
This belief there has to be more to life and things can't be so dim,
All about alignment with source and the golden light within,
I remember driving through the city thinking I am so lost,
I feel a pain inside my heart that not even heaven can abort,
I hate this place, I hate you too, I hate it all - I am stuck,
In this disillusioned abyss and a plain old rut,
What I came to be shown by the world is that you weren't even real,
I'd made you up in my mind to escape my own fortune wheel,
I couldn't love myself enough so I needed you for the void,
A recipe for disaster is the only way to explain this disgraceful ploy,
I was lying to myself about the truth, a disservice to you too,
That you were coming in like a knight and shining armour to save me from the pool,
The pool of drowning in black tides where my soul was drowning fast,
In the pain of the past and the pain of the present - I wouldn't have made it last,
I realised I needed to get my own life raft and help myself breathe for air,
You were never coming to get me, it was a sin and to much of my despair,
I realised why would I even want someone else to come?
Save me like I needed anything except my own divine,
I started looking inside myself and understanding where it all went wrong,
Why wasn't I feeling love and in my own personal hell,
Probably since birth I lacked because of fate's choice,
My power lied in my own sense of self worth,
Rising from the ashes and dust like a phoenix does with choice,
My powerful might has helped me rise into a person of my own worth,
I now drive through the city looking for adventures and rebirth,
I realised in this journey on earth so many things stray us from the path,
But really all they do that for is to teach us what we failed to understand from the start,
We are own alchemist, our own one true companion and love,

Once we realise this notion the divine enters from up above,
It gives us everything we need to slay the demons of the night,
To rise and conquer wars within ourselves and tyrant through the fight,
We live to see another day and love ourselves even more,
That's when the universe comes in and hits the floor,
Delivering all the blessings, abundance and the goods,
That we deserved from the start, if only we had understood,
The journey home's a funny one and beautiful at that,
We rise from the ground into divine accepting everything that got us there,
Even if the heinous crime was beyond our own despair,
It's ok to look back with compassion for what you didn't know,
Before you realised what you needed to obtain your Holy glow.

Sew Those Dreams Girl

There's a powerful notion in manifesting your dreams,
Like everything you see you were the creator with the sewing machine,
You were able to sit with pen to the paper at hand,
And write a vivid list of all your demands,
The ones you wanted and had no doubt in sight,
That they were your heavenly birth right,
The ones that you knew would fulfil your soul,
The ones that you feel like would bring you to your sense of whole,
Until you realise you're already there,
You just sit with patience knowing what you want is on it's way and being birthed
right into plain sight thin air,
The fruition begins to collaborate with your day,
You taste the fruit you once did dream of as you lay,
You now realise the power of your dreams.
To hold what you seek in the palm of your hand,
To grow to new heights and let the universe lay down the demands,
This way of living becomes a birth right, as you soar to new divine heights,
You realise living in fear is a low way to go, It helps you achieve nothing and steals
the soul and its glow,
The magic and power of knowing your own worth,
Is shown from heaven with a divine sense of gifts from the earth,
Revel in the glory that is the blessing in divine,
You deserve it and thousand ways to smile more than time to time.

A Sinner's Hell, A Saint's Dream

The fear of finding out the truth,
Is far less painful than the fear of being denied your youth,
Holding yourself hostage to a soul that binds,
One where you are unable to find your nirvana and sublime,
One where you're trapped down to the core,
Hearing broken promises and finding hells floor,
The moment you choose to rise from the trap,
Is the moment they come crawling wanting you back,
Like everything they'd done had left no scar,
Like everything they'd done had not broken your love,
But here's thing thing that needs to be faced,
That everything you feel is not a mistake,
It's to transform your pain and take you to a new place of love,
A new heightened understanding of the world from above,
A way to face the sorrows of your past,
A way to break the chains that make this hurt last,
If you face the anger and the tears,
You'll be able to rise from all the dis ease,
And in this glorious moment,
A brand new rebirth is chosen,
One where you surrender to the past,
One where you observe it and it doesn't last,
For the pain is a messenger to your dreams,
Not a chain that binds you at the seams,
This ascension helps you soar to new worlds,
Paradigms, the astral plane, and pearls,
You're able to let go of the grasp you hold on tight,
And surrender into the day and the night,
Knowing what is meant for you will come,
Knowing that you no longer have to numb or run,
For when you release the sadness and grief within,
It is you who truly does win,
You transmute the change into self love that helps you rise,
Rising higher than any emotion ever touched by anyone except the wise,
Into a new paradigm with all that is,
Into self forgiveness and a new abyss,
This is where you'll find your treasure,
The one that you were born to find beyond measure,
This paradise is bliss and a new found freedom from within,
A sinners hell and a saints dream.

Let Go

How do you let go of someone you thought was the one?
The one that had came to finally give you love,
The love in return you always give yet never got back,
Leaving you high and dry - like a solider with no tact,
It's easier said than done and takes some time,
But in the end you'll surely find,
That you needed none of what they even had,
All you needed to focus on was what you felt like you lacked,
Inside your soul and inside your heart,
You are your own divine counter part,
Nobody could ever come to fill the place,
The one where you fill yourself with love and divine grace,
This place inside is deep like a wishing well,
Where you inner child is at the bottom yelling out for help,
You reach down and offer them a helping hand,
Spreading love and kindness without a single judgement or demand,
You let them know how deep they're loved,
That no matter what happens you're here to send help from above,
You've got their back no matter what the cause,
You're here to show happiness and help them follow their steps back to self worth,
To show themselves compassion and love beyond depth,
To hold their hair back when they're feeling repressed with fear,
To let them know they know they're worth more than gold,
To love them harder than any curse limitation could hold,
They now rise to the table of the kings,
To find themselves shining from within,
This glorious rise to self love,
Is one the sun shines down from up above,
This moment of freedom allows the light to shine,
Deep within the soul of the one that is divine.
You've conquered all the beasts and monsters within,
You've let go of people who project their sins,
This rise to the top will surely find,
You are worthy of a million pieces of love reflected on the outside.

How do you silence fear, do you tell it to go?
Do you look it in the eye and tell it your woes?
Do you send it love or do you invite it in?
Do you welcome the pain and let it dim heavens glim?
For sometimes I feel it comes by itself,
It shows up uninvited, like you're at the dinner party to hell,
You're trying to kick it out of the royalty seat,
But it comes and stays and puts up its feet,
Why is it that trauma helps us write so free?
Why is it that pain is what I feel when I look at thee,
All these questions like a circus I'm in,
Well I packed up and left the circus and chose to let go of this sin,
I told fear to vacate the premises and to leave my mind,
I told it, it was uninvited and it's perpetrated a crime,
I told it to get up and get out of my house,
For I packed this whole circus and left this townhouse,
I chose to focus on the love within,
I silenced the monsters and demons that showed up with their kin,
Once I took this power I sent it all light,
I focused on the good and the magic inside,
What I surely did find is the more I focused on love,
Flowers grew instead of monsters in my head up above,
The flowers allowed bloom as the seasons changed,
You should have seen when summer came it changed all the pain,
It helped me realise that there's a light from within,
It never goes out and it never gets dimmed,
It's an eternal solar powered source that sits deep in your chest,
It reminds you of your holy self and divine grace and does bless,
It kicks out the pain no matter what time of day,
It shines greater than heaven on a cloudy day,
Once you turn on this light it's a magical touch,
The rest of the world mirrors you and you find yourself thriving and lust,
You find love all around and getting noticed by it all,
You find yourself heavy on attention from ones who deserve your glow,
You rise from the ashes and out of the dust,
You become a Queen of your life and help those who don't trust,
This entire shift has changed your paradigm and sight,
For all three of your eyes are open now and you find a new sense of flight,
This plane ride to a new vibration has shifted your mind,
You're able to glow to new places and grow against the illusion of time,
Your own love becomes a catalyst of happiness from within,
The entire good world around you becomes like a moth to your glim,
You glimmer so bright and you spread so much love,
You're worth all the diamonds from heaven above,
Once you learn how to silence the monsters upstairs,
Heaven will send you gifts like you're the Queen of Bel Air.

When you flow with life you allow it in,
You become a loving breathing thing,
You are in a state of receiving and resistance it goes,
Far away into the dreamy unknown,
For when you're standing tall like a flower in the grass,
You're flowing with the wind and ready to see the winds pass,
You're enabling all aspects of life to be,
Allowing things to flow within and with peace,
This state of being raises your vibration,
Enabling the opportunity for all you seek to manifestation,
This state of being is the only way to receive,
It's the epitome of God flowing through the wind and the trees,
It's the answer to the questions you seek so far,
The ones you pine over and wonder where they are,
For when you let go of the notion it becomes to clear,
You're in a state of allowing for your manifestations to appear,
Scream into the universe that which you seek,
Then let go of the mountain and watch its peak,
Return to you when you least expect in the divinity of time,
Gifted from the universe like the hands of our loving life,
Handed to you and through you for it can be no other way,
That everything you seek will be returned to you on the right day,
This is the key or the castle that you seek,
Speak your truth and elevate your peace,
Allow things to flow towards you like they magnetise your soul,
For this is your birth right, you only true hold,
You have ascended in awareness once you've grasped this down,
Knowing everything you seek can beautifully be found,
A simple notion nobody taught us since birth,
But here it is freely given to you,
Heaven upon earth.

Rise Child

Here it is all that you seek,
Right before your eyes ready to hit its peak,
Now you realise all you had to do,
Was surrender it back to the universe so it can arrive for you,
This magical notion has surely found,
It's way back to you like a Queen and her crown,
Believe you deserve it and the universe will serve it,
This understanding brings a soul peace,
Knowing all they're required to do is sit back and expect it in,
They're waiting for its presence to come,
Having faith that everything they seek is on its way to them,
Without a moment of doubt and faith at their hand,
They'll have desires at their own command,
For it's the law of the universe delivered in it's glory,
A holy essence upon us mortals growing into divine stories,
Our ways and our notions are finding our power,
Through our solar plexus the universe will shower,
Unto us our glory that which we seek,
It's the highest understanding of man's knowledge leaked,
We are our own God standing at the edge of a cliff,
Speaking unto the universe everything we do seek,
Waiting for the waves to return upon us now,
The gifts of the world that which we bestow,
We are powerful energy upon this divine earth,
Once we understand and see our own worth,
For this magic beneath us surely helps us find,
Peace in the knowing we create through our minds,
So pour out your heart child and speak out your truth,
And let go of it throughly and focus on your youth,
Focus on the the things that keep your spirit wild,
And watch the universe deliver everything you ever dreamt mild,
For now you're understanding the powers in your mind,
You've knocked down the towers that do bind,
You to old belief systems and lower vibrations,
As you've arrived here at the holiest station,
Rise child to the dreams you aspire,
For it cant be any other way except all you aspire.

The Magician

The damages that happened were lessons not punishments,
For the mind is a powerful weapon of destruction,
For if it is not controlled or focused unto that which you seek,
It can run havoc and cause mania on earth which you didn't intend to peak,
This engraved notion that you hold dear to your heart,
The one you which to create and the dreams you seek to start,
All they require is your attention and focus,
For where focus goes energy does flow,
Creating a sequence of events because of that thought,
So why not focus on all the things that do not distort,
Your power and your gains and shift away from the past,
For today's the only day you can create things that last,
Let go of the old chapters and forgive all those wounds,
Stop playing with the thoughts and observe them without wound,
Stop playing the protagonist in your story,
Release the thoughts beliefs and notions that do not raise you to your glory,
You're a creature of magic, a magician at hand,
Anything you seek to create you can do so at your demand,
You're a master magician and everything you think,
Will arrive at your doorstep with a top hat and glass eyed wink,
For you create your reality whether you realise or not,
So focus on what you want and not on that which you do not,
It is a simple notion and one that without doubt,
Can bring you anything you desire, even more than hard work cannot,
This quantum physics energy is what you're made of,
Like a silver present box filled with a magicians wand,
You are what you seek, and you're the answer to your prayers,
Let go of your doubt and have faith in the hand,
That's being delivered to you,
So get out of your manifestations way,
And allow the state of receiving to become the brink of the day,
Focus on the things that raise your vibration,
For now you've arrived at heavens station,
Oh creator of the divine, don't you see your power?
From the moment you were born you belonged from heavens tower,
You are allowed to have it all,
Don't listen to a single soul who tries to rip it from your core,
Let your light shine upon this earth,
Know your divine sense of worth,
You will rise to the top and hold it all in the palm of your hand,
Enjoy the ride whilst the universe blesses your commands.
A love story, home to yourself.

The Breaking Open

How do you know if something is dead?
Are you inside yourself full of dread?
Do you think the pain is deep within,
Or is it a catalyst for all your dreams,
Sometimes we don't know what's on the other side,
Because its where we've never been,
We can't see the double side of the coin,
Because we're the ones that are breaking open from inside these chains,
How do we know the other side of where we are going isn't better than where we've been before?
How do we know the other side doesn't lead to an open door?
How are we to know what's gone is better than what's to come?
How do we know if we don't surrender to the unknown,
The breaking of the wound is where the healing begins,
For the pain seeps out like poison from our lungs,
It bleeds into the sky and distances itself from us,
It leads us to the abyss and helps us rummage through the rough,
It forces us to surrender and to live without despair,
For holding those ten swords would just cut us beyond repair,
So before we fly we are asked to bleed,
For in the bleeding and the releasing it's where we feel at ease,
We are reborn unto ourselves, unto love,
Where we find this holy light within us that shines from up above,
For when we break open and open our shell,
We are reborn out of the pits of hell,
We fly high, like a butterfly out the cocoon,
We rise up far and leave these empty wounds,
It is here where we rise and we are free to go out wild,
Where we have never been into the deeper recesses of our inner child,
We will find a secret paradise one of portal and immediate bliss,
Where we can rise unto love again and let go of these painful things,
And in this breaking open we are reborn,
Unto love like the dying are given another thorn,
Another chance at life, another shift or perspective,
Like the ancient Egyptian scripture talked about these blessings,
For in the book of the dead they speak about life,
As if you were reborn unto this holy night,
Only the magicians find this gracious ease,
And so to you my friend, so welcome the grief,
Let it find itself a home within you temporary listen to what it has to say,
Then send it away and be merry today,
For honouring and releasing invites the rebirth,
And unto this holy night you shall feel a new earth.

Children

The children are our innocent protege at best,
It's our job eternally to protect them and keep them free from harms nest,
They are the future of this world and they hold the power to the revolution,
We are to treat them like our kin, but salute them like our leaders,
They hold the gifts from the angelic realm above,
One which will deliver freedom to hell on earth and its rummage that's turned rough,
They are here to shift these paradigms and show us where we are unfree,
For in the children lie the next available beauty within this earths reach,
They are the magicians and the rainbows that are set upon this world,
To shed light to the darkness and speak of beauty's untold,
They hold magic in their bones and they deliver us from sin,
They will write tails on this earth to allow the revolution to begin,
For the beauty of the inner child is where we really begin,
To eliminate pain and illuminate sin,
We will highlight our wrong doings and free ourselves from pain,
To heal ancestral trauma is where we need to start to gain,
Perspective on how and why we ended things so wrong,
Why money goes to the Middle East and all these monster bombs,
Why are people suffering? Why can children starve?
Why are we all out of balance and the politicians have the power?
For people have yet to learn their own power,
That through their mind they can heal their words and manifest their desire,
They can shift their world and raise their lives if they're educated through,
All that needs to happen is a conversation with their baby too,
Their own inner child the one that yearns for help,
The one that's lacking nourishment and been neglected since birth,
This world is unbalanced and the children hold the key,
To come and revolutionise the pain that people feel,
To show them where they're lacking and to show them where they're hurt,
To help them raise their vibration and rise like flowers from the dirt,
I pray for this earth and peace and for the people to rise to power,
For the children hold they key and the desire to start this fire,
This fire in our hearts that will change the hands of time,
Even though it's a man made illusion in this paradigm,
For this world is magic and this world is bigger than the box it's made,
The one where people lay down and they are constantly betrayed,
By their leaders and the government and the people in control,
Feeding them lies, manipulating their fear and treating them so cold,
Where's the medical? The help? Where's the money in the pandemic?
Can't you lend a helping hand to those who suffer and have nothing?
The children will change this world, in kingdoms to come.
For everything the sinners have done will one day come undone.

Perfect Sunday

The Sunday that speaks volumes to me,
Is one where I lay under the oak tree,
In a garden by the flowers, Sitting besides my love and my house,
By the sea that speaks of peace and harmony,
In vibration and alignment with all that is,
I look around and see my eyelashes flutter,
I feel the depth and warmth of the sea breeze, melts like butter,
Feeling that knowing deep down in my heart,
Is the beauty and the magic, feels like magicians art,
How was I so lucky to get here and how come God chose me,
To teach me the magic of the universe and support my dreams with ease,
He got me good and lifted me higher,
I remember sitting in my room year after year crying,
Wondering if he's forgotten me and wondering what I'd done wrong,
How was a child meant to suffer for so long and so strong?
But what I came to realise once the pain had sufficed,
That it was never meant to last and was meant to shatter the ice,
Break down the shards of illusion that I was trapped in these memories of pain,
And shoot me like an arrow into the depths of my own personal gain,
I'm like a bird with wings that fly higher than a mountains peak,
I'm like a sultan who holds every key to every door in the kingdoms lease,
I am free from those chains that bind,
Laying here by the flowers on a Sunday with my lover in the sunshine,
Thank you God - for it all - the pain and all the blessings,
For not knowing the other side of the coin,
I wouldn't be able to constitute this abundance,
The honey wouldn't taste so sweet and the love wouldn't feel so fire,
Like every inch of my soul has been yearning with desire,
I'm finally home to myself and I have myself to thank,
Everything else surely followed me like a coin in my money bank,
I'm so full of love like every cell was created to be free,
How do I even express to you the gratitude that lay beneath my feet,
I am finally at the expense of my own desires,
Because I had faith and never doubted you not even when there were towers,
That fell and crushed my soul like it was the day that I would die,
I looked to the sky and said I know you're here by my side,
I cry even writing this thinking I couldn't have made that choice,
That temporary decision with a permanent ending point,
But I didn't ever lose faith and I never stopped to do it,
Because all I kept thinking about was the heaven that got me through it,
I thought of laying awake at night with angels cradling my soul,
Healing every inch of pain like they sponged it out of my hearts hole,
Our focus is so powerful and gets us through despair,
A Sunday built from heavens touch because I came up to gasp for air,
Gratitude is underrated and gets you through it all,

Like the magic beneath this now moonlight,
Shining on my lovers skull,
I love this world and shifted mindset to focus on the light,
For if you choose to see darkness everywhere it sucks you in without delight,
Choose to see the love and light that exists within us all,
It will lead you to magic and mountains and help you retain gold.
A Sunday afternoon with my lover.

Voids Are An Illusion

How come everyone tries to fill the void?
Why do they run from the pain and avoid the noise?
I'd been surrounded by the karmic souls,
People who linger taking hold of the ones I love the most,
They have intentions that aren't love and they're not even great,
They use the people I love and lure them in like they're bait,
How come all the people I love can't see what I see?
Why can't they realise their worth and let go of these schemes,
Why does someone else have to make them feel grand?
Why does someone else have to fill their souls demands?
How come they don't love themselves more than enough,
Why are they looking around to spend time with someone to feel love,
Is it my own self that needs to forgive myself too?
For accepting karmic souls before I learnt better than to?
For at the end of the day i'd rather walk alone,
Than have another person touch my soul with their hands that are unknown,
Unknown to themselves and unknown to the truth,
Walking around filling their void too,
This is how people end up so damaged because they are in relationships that don't serve,
They swerve the self work and end up hurting everyone in loads,
They end up leaving and projecting for they don't know their own,
They end up in karmic unions creating hell upon earth,
But it's without judgement I say this it's more cause I care,
That the people I love so dearly are surrounded by less than a breath of fresh air,
I'm just grateful I ascended past judgement into love,
It's just sometimes trying to care for them, realising there's heaven up above,
They're on their own journey and they have to learn,
Whether they choose to or not is their cross to bear hold,
I'm waiting still in my power to meet other souls,
Who have risen through their trauma and have each other's hands to hold,
I've seen it far and few and I know it exists,
So here I am talking about it manifesting it,
I want those people I love so much to flourish and win,
I pray for their abundance and their rising from the people who sin,
God protect those on earth and the ones that I love,
Help them see what I see, their shining light from up above.

The Emptiness

How to fill the emptiness deep inside?
Is it an illusion or do you run and hide?
Do you find yourself looking for anything else to do,
Do you find yourself trapped without options too?
Do you eat it, smoke it and drink it away?
Do you find yourself trapped in these painful grief stricken ways?
For you if you just shift your focus to the present not the past,
If you focus to right now where you're here right on this path,
And you silence your mind and control your own thoughts,
You rise above the ashes, let go of the ten of swords,
You stay present in this moment releasing unwavering doubt and fear,
You're able to crash tackle the courses of tears,
You focus on this moment and silence all those thoughts,
Continue to do so and watch your vibration shift all sorts,
You start to feel calmer and deeper at peace,
You realise your mind is creating a weapon of grief,
So stay focused on this moment and realise your own self,
That you derive from an ocean of love not a drop in a wishing well,
You're almost getting better and you've got it down pact,
You find yourself running from anything that feels less than that,
You are able to rise without grief in your heart,
Finding passion and power and knowing when to start,
Your journey in this earth with love in your heart,
All because you shifted your focus just back to your minds heart,
Get out of your head and into your heart,
Know your own self and your divine counter part,
For what you focus on is what you create it's the universal law,
Shift away from giving your energy to the ten of swords.
Coming home to yourself.

Storm

There's a storm that rolls in sometimes on a sunshine day,
It's confusing to the weather man as he thought the forecast wouldn't change,
There's not much you can do when things revel in upheaval,
The shadow's of the clouds silhouette against the suns reflection,
The rain on a summer's day,
Astrological nonsense,
Like the tides shifting when the moon is at a stand still,
It happens when you least expect it,
Coming over you like a hawk,
Prepare yourself for the bigger brighter future where you'll soon depart,
Away from the rain and into the light,
Provided you take shelter and allow the rain to take flight,
Just for a little while honouring its presence,
Like the steam from the hot wet air will linger in essence,
This too shall pass you tell yourself as your engulfed with this confusion,
You stand in your power after as the rainbow has come to fruition,
You knew the time would come when this moment would pass,
But in the meantime the discomfort surely felt like it did last,
Remember to know that everything you think and feel isn't kosher,
Sometimes it's just the wheel turning towards the next chapter,
Embrace the winter and the summer all seasons wrapped up in one,
Because one day sweet child the sun will come,
And in this sunshine you will revel,
Feeling every inch of your body filled without grievance or upheaval,
It will be like not a moment has even passed besides,
Now it doesn't even matter your life has become your art,
For your the Picasso with the paintbrush,
The master to the piece,
The author of the title,
The one who directs the film piece,
Allow this to inspire you and create your own solidarity and dreams,
For your life dear child is really all that it seems.

Light Inside

The fire inside me surely does burn,
It turns me inside out and turns my head to a storm,
How do I calm these waters is it plain to see?
That everything I sought after is seeking me?
Why can't I silence the thunder and storms,
Why can't I find this benevolent peace upon all these thorns?
Have I found myself truer than most and stuck in this trap,
Or is it just my head inside telling me that I do lack?
Am I free from the pain? Or does the power and peace,
Lack their own resistance to fall upon my feet.
I deserve these blessings I know it in my heart,
But how do I make these negative thoughts depart?
Do I find the freedom in my own true will,
Do I find myself letting go of the chains I'm tied to,
I'm tired inside me, not even fatigued,
My soul is yearning for this deeper internal peace,
But here I stand in awareness knowing there has to be more,
More than this pain and more than I've ever felt before,
Do I proper and come up to this own sense of will,
Or will heaven release me from these chains I'm built to,
I realised through asking the questions were heard,
They were filled with such power behind all my words,
I started to understand that maybe everything I think,
Comes to fruition at the universal brink,
Like how do I hear my own thoughts mirrored to me?
How do I find solace and peace within every inch of me,
I learnt to understand the deeper meaning of life,
By getting out of my head and feeling every inch of my heart,
The conscious mind was dragging me deeper in its hold,
I got out of there and ran for cover in the circumference of my heart's gold,
For in there it knew the answers to my prayers,
I heard whispers not loud cries, not making demands,
It freed me and taught me to learn to love and feel peace,
To flow with the energy and let go of resistance and keep,
Keep a hold of the regrets the chains that bind,
The past mistakes that no longer I find,
I no longer find myself trapped in this idea of what's gone,
Like I lost out on something or lacked something and got torn,
I realised every moment I was creating a new,
Whether I was present focused or not,
I had a job to attend to,
It was to silence my brain and focus on something else,
Something in that present moment to return to great health,
For now I had become in a state of peace, an allowing, a receiving,

For everything I do wish,
And in this wishing and hoping I found love at heart,
I realised that everything now was a magnet towards my griefs depart,
I am now living my true authentic divine self,
All because I had the power and courage to silence what no longer helped,
If we are able to focus for a period of time,
Consecutively the universe will deliver everything we do dream of and overthinking was our crime,
Let go of it all and just learn to be,
For the freedom is magic and a divine wishing tree.

Align

The beauty in arriving home once and for all,
Just got to be ready to embrace the change and transform your soul,
Nothing you need exists outside of your own,
Your own sense of awareness, your body, your home,
When you are able to balance and process your emotions first,
You're able to balance the divinity that exists around this world,
For it isn't until you balance your thoughts,
That the universe begins to deliver all sorts,
All sorts of blessings of that which you seek,
All sorts of love from heavens peak,
Everything you want is heading towards you fast,
If you're able to control your thoughts and focus more than the last,
For manifesting is all about understanding the will,
The will of your intention and focusing it to kill,
Any doubts, any fears of your dreams,
You need to get out of the way in of that which you seek,
Get out of your head and into your heart,
Know your one with the divine and you deserve to play the part,
Once your are able to silence your thoughts,
The divine delivers the goods like you're waiting for your severed parts,
The parts of you that were taken from your God given rights,
The parts of you that didn't blossom like you divine birth right,
You're a product of the fire,
A blossom of the earth,
A fragile being in nature deserving to be heard,
So silence those thoughts and get out of your way,
Let those you desire in your universe make their way,
To you beloved, as such you deserve,
For everything you seek is as easy as a flying bird,
He opens his wings and trusts that he'll soar,
And once he takes the first step,
A thousand will follow more,
So be deserving and ready to receive that of which you seek,
For it can be no other way when you silence the fears,
This is your divine birth right,
Your one true ascension from above,
Learn the powers of this universe and teach them for eternity like a white dove,
Soars high in the sky knowing her divine worth,
Enjoy this life here on this fragile earth.

The beauty that you find from focusing on the thoughts,
That make flowers from the bloom instead of storms from the doubt,
Grows into an inundated blessing that grows you to a new self,
Every time you walk outside you emit new frequency to earth,
When you raise your thoughts, you raise your vibration,
Everything that meets you in your day holds new fruition,
Science has shown us that this is to be true,
That everything you seek in your vibration is seeking you,
Go up to that high vibrational kingdom and find your own worth,
Know yourself so deeply and let go of all the distort,
Let go of the chains that tie you to the floor,
The ones that show you and tell you're nothing and you're not worth more,
These preconceived illusions were generationally passed down,
They no longer serve you or your giant crown,
You're here to grow to soar above the sky,
To help change this earth,
To raise that vibration,
To fly high,
This peace and this new found freedom within,
Helps you recognise everything else before was a lie and you're own sin,
Untrue and contrary to popular belief,
Depression is real, Only if you believe it to be,
Spinning in your head like a hamster on a wheel,
When you face that deep trauma,
Say goodbye to the grief,
You're able to let go and fly your kite higher than the reef,
Higher than anything you ever have known,
Breaking this cycle and pattern takes time to disassociate yourself from the woes,
To rise like the King or Queen you were sent here to be,
To free yourself from a life of anything but ease,
This takes time coming home to yourself dear love,
Be gracious with ease,
Be patient on your soul and learn to take the keys,
Back to the kingdom the one where you'll reign,
You'll get out of your own way and raise to fame,
Once you understand it all begins in your mind,
The power to life is here to make find,
You're an alchemist and a lover,
A powerful sorcerer at best,
No longer settle for second best and say goodbye to the lack,
For now what you think you create,
What you tell yourself in your mind,
Shows up for you in your state,
So focus darling on what it is you wish to create,
Master your day and paint the brush to the palate.

Risen

Rise, like the day only serves you at best,
Like everything you want and need is coming to you in the divine timing's best,
You're a wanderer of this earth like we all are too,
You're wondering how did you get here and what's required of you,
What if I told you that you're already serving your purpose,
If that stranger you smiled at, the person you showed love,
Was your purpose being met,
We all search far and wide like there's more to be done,
Just be still child and feel the light of the sun,
Listen to the inner knowing the intuition you have,
It is your compass on earth and will guide you for days to come,
Towards that which your meant to be with and that which is your soul,
Towards the way in which you will prosper and the lessons will be told,
You're rising like a Phoenix from the ashes,
Like an ascending soul to the brim,
Of happiness, joy, compassion and fulfilment,
You have so much to see and nothing to do,
Just be still child and let life flow through you,
Everything you seek is already here,
Everywhere you are, paradise is there,
You're an alchemist so focus your thoughts,
On sunshine and happiness and that which will not destroy,
You now are waking up to your oneness with the earth,
That everything exists through you and create your divine birth,
There are no others and nothing exists without us,
For everything we feel and think we manifest like bones and dust,
We see this magic in alchemy and we start to understand,
That what we think we create and what we know we demand,
We are now creating consciously the life of our dreams,
I am rich, I am happy, I am joyful, I am seen,
Everything you want in this life belongs to you,
Everything that you seek is also seeking you,
It's a simple notion but when it's down pact,
You balance your emotions and get out of the lack,
If you want everything to be delivered to your soul,
You just have to be ready and turn down any doubt it is yours,
For what happens now is you see what you think you create,
So only focus on positive things and don't give doubt the bait,
You're a magician now you realise your power with ease,
Only heaven will reward you with the birds and the bees,
Rise to your kingdom,
Rise to your sun,
Rise and rebirth,
Oh holy divine one.

Polarity

Balance is a concept not many understand,
They find themselves focusing on the things that they do not hold in their hands,
This illusion of lack creates seeds of fear,
Like planting a flower unto the Dead Sea,
Nothing will grow and everything wont work,
Why would you even try to prosper when your desires are destined to fail from the start?
Can't you see this power you hold in your hand?
Can't you see your divine worth and the gifts where you stand?
Can't you see that all that's required is for you to stand up?
Start thinking about planting seeds that reap rewards you can touch,
You need to focus on the things that serve your best at heart,
And let go of the fury, the pain, the departed and the rough,
You realise that everything that's happened is already gone,
Whether it was five seconds ago or a decade has passed,
This present moment is all you have,
What are you focusing on creating? Love or lack?
Focus on planting seeds of joy and prosperity,
For you cannot fail divine child, it is the laws in the streets,
It's the laws of the land, laws of the world,
Laws of the universe with so many stories untold,
Everything that you want already belongs to you to hold,
Raise your vibrations and your demands too,
Stop living in lack and know your divine place,
You're heaven on earth and such a divine race,
This alchemy is magic and soon to be known,
For now you can reap seeds of heaven and not that of woes,
Focus your thoughts only on what you want,
Tell those negative outcomes to go and rot,
They don't belong in your head and the past is dead and gone.
You are here now divine child,
Focus on the fun,
Focus on love, giving, joy, things you can't touch.
Things that make your soul glow a divine rush,
This happiness inside of you is all that you need,
For now you're siting under the wishing tree,
Creating the life of your dreams, Isn't it magic?
Now that you know? Go tell your neighbour who feels all the woes,
Go tell your mother whose heart never healed,
Go tell your father, Focus on the feels,
You're an amazing creature,
We all are on earth,
Just learn to turn down those negative thoughts,
And trust in your divine worth.

A Love Letter To My Inner Child

Hello dear child, It's been a long time,
Do you remember me? I'm your own protege in your mind,
I'm your creator and I'm now in charge,
I'm sorry I've neglected you and let you live amongst the shards,
I know you've been suffering in silence inside,
I know you've forgotten your divine worth dear child of mine,
It's no-one to blame I just didn't know more,
Nobody taught me better to love you and to hear you roar,
I realise now more than ever that you need my divine hand,
You need me to come and get you you're drowning in quick sand,
You need my attention and my love and my care,
You need me to listen and you need me to hold back your hair,
Whilst you purge out the pain and the grief you have felt,
The tales and tribulations of all the trauma you did receive and the belt,
To your face, to your head, to your heart, your parents did give,
Even though you have soon learnt to forgive,
As you've realised it wasn't their fault,
They too knew no better and were suffering as a result,
You loved yourself so dearly when you came out as a seed,
Now at thirty you're finding it hard to breathe,
I realise now more than ever I need a paper and pen,
To hear what you have to say and free all this sin,
You're so beautiful, you know that?
You're a divine goddess at bay,
Like a mermaid with a trident ruling under the sea today,
All of the love you never received,
Is buried within me and ready to be express delivered to you with ease,
For now is your time to rise unto the sun,
To let that love glow through your veins and rule number one,
You came here to conquer and conquer you shall,
I will my spend my life making sure of it and controlling the vows,
The ones that make sure you and your ancestors will live a life of love,
You'll win every race, You'll touch everything magical to touch,
It is my divine duty to protect you until we perish from this earth,
Now is the time dear love of mine,
To return as salt to the dirt,
To rise from the fire like a Phoenix and prosper this earth,
This is our time dear love of mine,
To rule this magical turf.

Here we go little child,
You ready to rise? You ready to see the earth shifting new tides?
You ready to win and to glow from the gold,
Within you you'll shine like new tales are untold,
You'll shift your energy to a new divine place,
Of graciousness and happiness and forgiveness and faith,
All you need to do is learn to silence your mind,
Forgive your woes and sins,
And those of the ones you loved once upon a time,
For now is abundance and prosperity and truth,
Now is the the time to find your divine youth,
Have you thought about what makes your soul speak and what makes it roar?
Have you realised that grief is ready to bail out the door?
Have you noticed shifts upon this new earth of ours?
Have you realised your power and committed oaths and vows,
To proper and rise, To win and to be,
As you no longer need to seek as everything you seek will grow to you with ease,
Your time has come to shake off these tides,
To eliminate the pain and to rise above with love and with pride,
But not the prideful ego,
The one that held you back,
Just raise your head and know your worth and never look back,
For everything that you desire does desire you too,
Get out of your own way and negativity will decease from you,
You realise that all you need is to wake up and think,
Focus your intentions,
On the manifestation you expect to exist,
You focus your thoughts on unconditional love and support,
You understand your manifestations no longer are distort,
For now you realise that everything you want,
Is more than obtainable you just have to have a high vibrational resort,
This resort is where you gifts will be delivered,
Where you align with source and are ready to feel quivers,
That you are able to create just by thinking a thought,
Knowing you're provided for,
And waiting to be told,
That there's a ring of the doorbell,
The magic you ordered is here,
The freedom you sought is seeking you,
And everything is right again with peace,
But believing is the key and focus holds the lock,
This is a divine gift that you're ready to unlock,
So be able to understand to this notion,
And teach your children too,
They no longer have to lack and suffer,
They will rise and they will prosper and everything will come to them too.

The Butterfly

First your born in this cocoon upon earth,
You rise to the heavens and you'll realise your divine worth,
But before you get to this place you start like a worm in the dirt,
You have to see the darkness sprawled upon this unkind earth,
You realise you've never known anything more,
How long have I been in this darkness? How much more is there to endure?
Do I know anything else is there anything to feel?
What's happening to me and when does my fortune move this wheel?
The questions begin to shift the hands of time,
Move you towards lessons to move the cocoon into the sunlight,
For in the sunlight you realise there's more than the dark,
The an entire being of happiness in which to move towards to depart,
Depart from this cocoon of where I was born, one where I sat in the dark and cold and felt torn,
I start to feel this sunlight upon my dark skin,
But not everything happens immediately there's lessons and there's things to be seen,
There's things to be understood and time to find self,
Not everything can happen straight away and we need to focus on this earth,
What do we want to create and what is the life we seek?
How do we depart from this pain and this grief that lies in the cocoon within,
Is time to rise yet? Is it time to fly?
How we do move and jump and have faith and grow and soar to new heights?
It takes time to develop these wings and learn,
That all along inside of you, you held the tools to be torn,
Torn out of this cocoon and freed into this world,
To fly higher and soar to new heights and develop divine wings to help,
Now is the time you've realised to take that leap of faith,
Otherwise you'll stay in this cocoon and decease in this state,
You say goodbye to the darkness and free your own soul,
You love yourself deeper and harder and know you're ready to let go,
You jump, taking your first gasp of air,
Knowing that happiness exists within and there's no longer need to despair,
This is how you grow with your own wings of faith,
Transformation like the butterfly from a deceased state.

Tarot In Real Life

There's a moment in time when you begin to feel it,
A sublime sensation entails your entire being,
Like how have I never felt this peace of mind before?
How have I never been engulfed by this sun that I forgot I did adore,
How have I not let love touch my heart before,
How did I fall into the misery trap?
How did I let others bring my soul back,
Back to the ten of swords of misery they were feeling,
Like I was a part of their projection not their healing,
How could you let someone trap you back?
Do I feel gratitude or do I feel lack?
Do I have gratitude for the things that held me back?
Because they're the reason I'll never stop to think and fall,
I'll never stop a moment of anything except my peace once more,
I'll never let you take me back to hell where you reside,
I'll never let you touch my soul with your dirty hands and pride,
I'll never let you near me again with your engulfment and obsess,
I'll never let you shake my soul and take out my pentacles and my best,
I now have come home to myself and love myself so much,
For what I ended up learning was more than money could buy,
My vibration began to lower spending time by the devils side,
Why did I allow myself to go back and fall down again time after time?
We do crazy things when we feel connection, like this person could give us solace,
But what we find and what we remember is the key to our solar plexus,
Is in our own hands, Our power and our might,
Is through God and not another for that's to project your illusion into the night,
Our love is so powerful it comes from God's own source,
Our will is so powerful, It breaks the chains that tie us to a dead horse,
The moment that sun touches your skin you remember your divine worth,
You take the queen of swords and shatter everything that doesn't on this earth,
For what the lesson taught me was greater than anything that could bind,
That I am the high priestess and I am the love of my own life.

Freedom

The new is the state of mind that I would like to be,
In a new place of wisdom, peace, gracefulness, and ease,
I'm feeling winds I've never felt, Higher than ever before,
I'm aligning with source and heaven's belt knowing my own divine source,
I know now that everything that led me here was painful as can be,
Not to punish my soul and loosen my worth but to give me grace and ease,
I realise now more than life I'm feeling freedoms worth,
I'm realising now more than ever that I hold the key to this earth,
Anything I want and anything I need flows with ease to me,
As I am the magician on this earth who now holds the key,
This key is the only thing that I can have with ease,
Because I open and unlock each door that was always meant for me,
I'm in alignment with source and things flow and glow with ease,
As a result of letting go and learning to just be,
This magic and understanding took a lot to learn,
I walked the path hell where my feet would always burn,
Burn like blisters in my skin from the gracelessness of life,
Every single turn and every single person was hurting my soul throughout the night,
I realised so much after the last time I could cope with pain,
That everything I had ever known had so much for me to gain,
For what you see is the universe taught me it's lesson painful as can be,
That nobody would worship me until I learnt my worth inside of me,
It's a mirror you know - that simple notion,
What you see is what they see,
Everything is mirrored, There are no others, It's only you through me,
This understanding changed it all, My love, My money, My career,
That everything we touch and see is what we think and feel from within,
If we are yearning constantly for another to fill the void,
We tell the universe we lack and something's missing and that's what we create on earth,
If we feel penniless and constantly have fear about a lack,
The abundance we have as our birth right is just given up without tact,
For what we need to understand is as simple as can be,
The medicine exists inside us, We just have to dive deep,
Into our wounds, kissing each scab and telling our little selves,
That we don't need another or these diamonds or these pearls,
All we need is to know we are divine love,
We come from a holy source from heaven above,
We come from the embers of the fire we found out self alight,
We love ourselves so deeply and so true,
We are able to overcome and obstacle of painful experience too,
The strength within us is built from wooden boards,
Like we were meant to learn our worth before we could reap all the rewards,
We are the Holy, The gifted loves, The beauty in plain sight,
We are the God given humans knowing our divine rights,
Now we rise to the top, We see who does come with,

All of the karmic souls that linger can stay beneath the weeds,
We have risen to new heights and understood our path,
Our divinity glows from our skin and breaks down all the shards,
We have risen to new senses and understood new depths,
Now the universe is delivering and pouring out its abundance,
Thank you for this magic I've created within me,
Thank you for teaching me my power and helping me see it from within,
Now I'll help others rise and teach them of their worth,
My souls purpose is being fulfilled and so is all my worth,
I love you God and I love this earth,
It's filled with magic and with love,
It's a heavenly place when you know you're worth,
You shine from up above like a diamond glow on earth.

Have you ever said thank you to the one who broke you most?
Have you ever looked back at your past and thanked those unholy ghosts?
Of the broken past and the painful glass that slit your own throat,
The ones that broke you down like monsters held you to choke,
Every last inch of you and every goodness out your eyes,
Like you couldn't breathe, you couldn't gasp and you had lost all your pride?
But like a Goddess you rose from the dead of the night,
You never lost any of your tact or your respect or your might,
Because you learnt with grace how to rise from the unholiest of places,
Like a fairy crawling out of a snakes cave without her wings after being maced,
You got up and could barely see both your eyes bruised and your heart torn,
Torn to pieces, shattered, by their unholy thorns,
You rose and repaired and hid in your slumber until your eyes could see,
Until you could remember who you were before they told you who to be,
This magic you still had within, was this a gift from God?
How could you still remember that this was inside you when you were raised in a
hell den without love,
How could you remember your worth and rise like a Queen to fly?
Even after everything you'd ever known, it would have killed someone else inside,
People don't even know what you had to do to survive and rise to where you are,
Not a single thing was given to your mental health besides painful scars,
You're on your way to rise to heaven and now you can see,
That this endurance you had learnt was not to suffer but to get you to where you
needed to be,
Like all these lessons catapulted you to heavens gate,
Like an arrow that shoots back before It gets shot to the target straight,
It's interesting this life, The ride can be a roller coaster too,
If that's your perception, that's your creation, that's your reality too,
So now I rise like a golden woman from heavens touch ,
Everything I felt previously like poison injected into my heart,
Was a lesson learnt and far removed, it feels like a past life,
Like I rose from the ashes into heaven like a bird with her own might,
Thank you for the lessons and thank you for the love,
I now feel a heavenly glow deep in my veins from up above,
Maybe one I'd never known if I had never felt hells woes,
I never thought i'd have gratitude for all of that pain I felt,
I almost took my own self from this world, but here I am and here I rise,
There's the ying and yang to life and the power that we see,
Is through the might we create and our third eyes glow with ease,
I am a divine gift from God, I know my heavenly worth,
I will rise like a Queen and will teach others upon the earth,
Their worth and their heavenly glow,
For what's a person if they don't share what they know to help others grow,
I know that's the point of life, The seed that's planted amongst earth,
Giving is really receiving and loving is really God's worth.

The Tide

The tides move and life changes, will you learn how to flow?
Will you learn how to make yourself obsolete from all that steals your glow?
Will you learn your depth and capacity and rise to standards of life?
Have you ever stopped to consider you divine holy birth right?
You're a magical being, you have so much power,
Has anyone told you your worth?
Do you even realise how Holy your presence is amongst the grains on earth,
Every single person on this earth has power and a divine might,
Their purpose here on earth is to level up and fly to heavens flight,
Every single thing on earth is sent like a gift from God,
For all of us to rise and flourish and learn our divine worth,
We are powerful beings and if we learn to persevere ,
We can do anything we wish and anything we please,
You see there are power in dreams and power in love and power in thinking good,
Those vibrations enter your temple and change the likelihood,
Of everything you've ever wanted and everything you've ever known,
When you feel like giving up the most, is when you should learn to keep to grow,
For there's lessons in this set back, and the come up never looked so bright,
Learning to have patience, gratitude and grace whilst your come up is on it's way
tonight,
You learn to ride the tides of life and learn to flow with it all,
You learn to keep moving yourself away from hells door,
Focus your intention on that which you seek,
Remember to silence and meditate and know your heavenly peak,
The negativity never got anyone anywhere they wanted to be,
So talk to yourself and tell your demons you're greater then they could ever be,
We all are going through it, Every single person on earth,
Now a single person at all has not felt this pain once before,
So rise like your sisters and brothers and guide each other home,
Learn your divine power and learn how to sacrifice those woes,
You're able to grow in your divine might and know your place to be,
You're a beautiful human with a beautiful heart and know where it is you need to be,
Silence your thoughts, turn on your heart, tune into the frequency,
What's it say, what's it feel, where do the tides lead you to be?
Follow these tides they hold they key to the castle,
The universe flows with these,
Even if everything in your might is frozen with fear and you freeze,
Unfreeze yourself and listen to that little child inside,
They know the way, they know the path no labyrinth can cause a fright,
You're the one who knows the way don't let the illusion cause a maze,
Your freedom lies in following the tides with grace.

To the one that got away,
Did they really swim so far?
Or was it illusionary from the beginning to think we own our counterpart?
What makes us believe someone else could come to us and sink,
Sink deep within our recesses like we own them to the brink,
We find ourselves trapped in this illusionary purge,
The place of purgatory the cathartic space, the one where we are held,
Deep in this state like another can fix our wounds,
Like that person that got away held the key to the tomb,
The tomb to unleash for the ancient book of the dead,
The rebirth begins and now we fear this dread,
This existential notion of purging and of loss,
Like that person belonged to us in the beginning and now we are pinned to our own
cross,
We bare the fruit of this earth and have so much power too,
We rise to kingdoms come and know our worth through,
Through this perceived notion of loss we learn and are able to see,
That everything we need exists inside and we are the ones who hold the key,
This notion is so powerful and it is so deep and so true,
That everything you seek inside is really seeking you,
You don't need another to fill any of your voids,
All you need is your power to take place and notice your own stance and ploys,
You realise now that everything you ever wanted existed from within,
And it was unholy and a sin like process to believe it would come from your kin,
Your own sense of self is mirrored in the world,
What a notion to believe you'd find it here on earth,
For what you've come to realise through purgatory and the loss,
Is that heaven threw you a bone in the coin toss,
You actually have everything you seek that lies within,
Your mistake was ever to believe another would take away that sin,
That painful ache and yearn you feel connection to the loss,
Is just a way to remind you of illusion in the coin toss,
Your beauty and your strength is given back with grace,
When you remember your divine self in this Holy race,
God is inside of you, you just need to tune in,
You need to remember that through your prayers you're able to seek it with him,
Never again will you ever believe another will fill your void,
For this is an illusionary rat race that takes you on a choice,
A choice top round through the wheel of fortune and travel round in flight,
Or to rise above the ashes like it's your divine birth right,
So now you realise that the one that got away,
Was sent from God to teach you to learn how to stay,
Stay in alignment with your source for nothing else is true,
Everything is just a mirror through me and through you.

There's a time on the journey where the frequency gap is too large,
Like nothing you say could contribute to them breaking the shards,
Sometimes the journey requires you to step away,
So people can see things in their own light of day,
You can speak a thousand words to the ones you love,
But sometimes it requires them to take the swords to themselves from up above,
Growth is a tricky thing that can cause dismay,
Being honest can seperate paths and change peoples place,
When you care so deeply and protect the ones you love,
Sometimes its misread because their the ones that need to learn from up above,
We all come here to work through the karma at hand,
Whether people realise it or not they're falling through quicksand,
When they ignore the obvious messages the universe makes them loud,
Until the illusion crumbles and there's no more sound,
Their words are not to be heard and the things they say don't find peace,
Because their tongue is tied to the piece of themselves they lost through the beast,
The one that they ignored when their world was coming down,
But they put up stilts and pretended they were on higher ground,
Life is funny when we live through the rose coloured glass,
How do you protect those you love? You don't, you step back and pray up above,
Heavens got them it's their path, take the higher ground,
Walk away and let them learn you can't save them they were destined to be found,
Sometimes you need to shed the skin of all people you once were,
In order to grow and reach new heights they can't all go to them its a blur,
This new level requires a maximum freedom one which you'll find,
Everything that was truly meant for you from the beginning of time,
Don't feel hatred, don't feel pain, don't feel resentment too,
Just let go gracefully of the things no longer meant for you.

Twin Flame

How do you tell the person that you love, that you know they love you too,
How do you tell the person that speaks no words, you hear them clearly too,
How do you tell the person that you're destined to become to let go and flow with ease,
When you know so much about your life and you're waiting to receive,
It's like you need to sit on your hands with temperance on your side,
Waiting for everything to be delivered to you and eliminate your pride,
You're just casually existing with no where to go or be,
You know that deep inside of you there's greater things to see,
You know that deep within your heart there's so much to be felt,
So many words but we have yet to break this dry communication spell,
How do you feel about this change, how do you prepare for it all?
Like you've missed your other half your entire life even though you're whole,
You realise deep inside your heart you need the freedom to,
To be alone and one with God before you're ready to,
To jump and take a leap of faith even though there's mild fear,
This love is greater than anything I've ever known and there's nothing else to see,
Everywhere I have gone to roam I have never found,
A love like this, a connection so strong, telepathic communication bound,
But you see what happens when the other person mirrors all your fears,
Is two beautiful souls scared to come home together and eliminate their tears,
It's a long journey home the one to self and every time i've found,
That everything I've needed was above higher ground,
God and the angels never left my side,
Working with me and my soulmate helping us eliminate our pride,
They told us on the astral plane that we were meant to be,
Even when we lived across the tides and the oceans seas,
We didn't even speak for years at a time,
But then there's this holy place inside my heart that knows we committed a crime,
We ignored what truly mattered and bottled up regrets,
We found our solace in our hearts but not walking earth steps,
I've come to realise life's too short why do we need to let it be,
When everything is not contort and our minds made it up to be,
It's pretty straight and simple, no matter where we've roamed,
The universe and God is showing there's no place like home,
Love is the most beautiful treasure on this golden earth,
I've loved you so much every single day since birth,
How did we get so lucky, did we wish upon a shooting star?
Did we find ourselves so blessed to find our divine counter part.

Mirrors

It's easiest to take out the pain on the ones we love,
Because they mirror our greatest insecurities and where we are unfree,
Instead of blaming others for our own choices,
Why wouldn't we look in the mirror to see?
There are no others, only one mirrored through all,
This tower that you climb the top of everyday just to fall,
Not even to your awakening and just to your own death,
Like the depths of hell can taste your soul and smell your sweet regret,
Why do we dislike the people who love us most when they try to save us from ourselves?
Is it because we're destined to feel these pits of hell,
You know they say that you can taste heavens touch until you've tasted hell,
Like you cant feel the love shine so bright until the demons fall,
I'm not sure how karma can come into such a drastic play,
Why do you need to fall down ten, thirteen, fifteen times a day?
Why can't you see things for what they are and realise your own worth,
Know immediately and straight away and see your own divinity on this earth,
Every time they treat you worse you choose you want to stay,
Like you've got nothing better going on in your life to save a demon today,
Is it us who needs to forgive ourselves for trying to save our loves,
Forgive ourselves for every time we did that to another before our rise above,
You wake up everyday and romanticise the one who hurts you most,
Like you keep needing to validate you're worth nothing and that it's them who'll boast,
The next time they slap your face or the next time they pull your hair,
The next time you fall down from grace and into the pits of despair,
I tried to help you a thousand times but still you fail to see,
Your own worth isn't sleeping beside a tragic karmic flea,
You need to remember your own strength and the best way to let this fall,
Is to walk away with no regrets and pray to God for more,
More justice, more awareness, more alignment too,
Your see when you rise, pray that your circle do that too,
They can't all come to the kingdom top, This is a painful lesson to be had,
The ones you love most may stay below and prove to themselves how much they lack,
Lack self love and strength and fill the void with pain,
For it's all the abuse has ever shown them there's drama to be gained,
I love you dearly and pray your growth but I will not take this reign,
For heaven is only experienced by people who want to gain ,
They wake up to their holy ness, they wake up to their worth,
Forgive themselves for every time they're unnecessarily chose to get burnt.
I love you for the divine creature that you are,
We ride together in a different space I'll always have your back,
But you chose to stay in the pits of hell where I chose to rise to live without lack,
Abundance and enlightenment is a choice not for the faint of heart,

For who better to hold yourself accountable as its been right from the start,
Your own self to have and to hold as long as you shall live,
Loving yourself is part of the journey there is no temporary fix.

When will we stop pleasing others and start living our divine path?
When will we stray from this notion that pain is all that lasts?
For there's beauty in the breakdown and there's God like love to be felt,
But everywhere I look around there's belting on this earth,
Good beautiful people filled with the faint of heart,
For they've been told since they were children that they were not a work of art,
They've been treated like average joes and given all the woes,
Abused since kids, narcissistic parents and neglect from their worth,
They find themselves tied down in life and attract people who reflect their worth,
Like everything they've experienced in life is just a negative hold,
Round and around the merry go around the one in which they lack,
But there comes a time when all the gravel needs to be chipped back,
Like the diamond needs to be driven out of the underground pounded concrete slate,
Once you start to see even a little glimmer from the ground of hope,
You rise in your might knowing that this was worth the work and float,
Float into an abundant energy of one where which you slay,
All of the negativity and the demons that do cross your day,
All of the negative thoughts and pain can linger from behind,
All of the beliefs that led you to your greatest crime,
That you forgot your worth, forgot who you are, forgot to come home to yourself,
You're a divine creature of this earth,
A child of the Gods,
One who is holy and free to rise from the shards,
Once you come home to yourself and see yourself for what you are,
There's not another person on this earth that can tell you who you're not,
So rise like the magic creature you came here to become,
Have compassion and self love on the journey home to thee.

How do you find balance when you dance with the devil?
Not the devil by religious standards but the one that draws you in,
Like a moth to a flame, they wrap you round and regain your sense of self,
They let you go and reel you in,
It's almost like a comfort that this insanity you know,
Has become a place that could feel like home,
A silhouette dance with the person who can grab your attention with the snap of their fingers,
I used to think this was love, this alluring hinder,
This karmic cycle and this born and raised rat trap,
Until one day I found myself alone with nobody who had my back,
Broken and confused with no where to feel at home,
I realised everywhere i'd been and everywhere I'd gone had only led me here,
To this empty place of loneliness and fear,
I realised that there's nothing to gain under the devils throne,
There's only an understanding that no place that feels like home,
So home became a new adventure too,
One inside my own soul finding solace without the pain and torture of you,
It was a glorious home with a safe space to be,
After living in the flames of the fire with the pain right next to me,
This peace was so kind to my gracious heart,
And chaos had left my life on its final depart,
I am so lucky to have made it, many of them don't,
They stay and set up shop and build a home,
Inside of the fire like it's their work of art,
Lying to themselves like they don't know how to depart,
From the painful cycle that never catches a break,
Just breaks their heart, spirit and soulful fate,
So now I reside in my temple of abyss,
And I seldom invite anybody in,
It's a magical place where I found my own love,
A beautiful home where fireworks go off on my own,
I know my own worth and love my own self,
I need not another to determine my throne,
Everything in this life is magic if you let it be,
Resisting the chain and nonsense of thought,
Haven't you played enough my dear?
You are welcomed to your own soul,
The place that you call home,
Here you reside on your own golden throne.

I wanna settle my mistakes,
But were they just life's greatest lessons?
Did I already align with source and learn my lessons?
Did I already find my own self worth through the painful blessings?
Where do I go from here and how do I find my feet,
Where do I find my self worth and how do I know what to think?
There's nothing to do and nowhere to be,
A silent voice inside my meditation whispered to me,
You just have to turn off all those thoughts,
That control you and run the show like a dark horse,
You're more powerful then anything you could ever know,
You just have to believe in yourself and silence the woes,
These magical thoughts you want to create,
Will shine out your face like sunshine in the day and the night,
You need to understand your mind controls it all,
Focus your intentions on nothing at all,
You'll raise your vibration and it will all come,
Everything that's meant for you without a single thing done,
You're the magician at hand and all you need to do,
Is silence your sadness and watch your progress zoom,
Towards you like its all you've ever known,
Follow your heart down a yellow brick road,
You're a magical person with beauty in your heart,
All that's required is you act like art,
Sit still in the silence and let it fill your soul,
You don't need an opinion anymore on anything so let go of your hold,
Trying to save others they can't even hear your screams,
Sometimes it takes letting go to align yourself with the life of your dreams,
You're a powerful sorcerer you didn't even know,
Now scream it from the rooftops to help others grow,
But don't be sad when the message is unclear,
That's their choice and journey to the pathway of eliminating fear,
Let that self love fill every cell of your bones,
Your journey was the progress to await your return home.

There's magic in the unknown,
It's where the madness does depart,
For what you have known previously was not the work of art,
That you knew your life could have been and now you've found yourself here,
Starting again from yourself and drinking your own tears,
You found your own source and no longer need another thing,
It took a long time to find this place but here you're in your strength and you win,
In such a divine grace with your own self to thank,
You look around and realise nobody knows what you're doing to get to this track,
Everyone's roaming around deep in their thoughts without themselves to hold onto,
We look for lovers like our parents,
And find ourselves in traps,
We haven't been taught our own divine worth and let go of all the crap,
The things that told us we aren't good and we need another soul,
To fill the void inside ourselves instead of nourish our own soul,
We're the masters and the magicians and the magic comes from within,
How can you have a bad day if another projects their sins?
We all are lost and wandering waiting to return home,
Trying to help others rise upon their thrones,
I learnt that voicing how you feel may break another's pride,
As they remain in their illusion on earth towards their stride,
It's a journey not for everyone and some you say goodbye,
For their own fate lies in the hands of their ego and their pride,
It's a funny world this place we live most don't get the goods,
They can't notice anything inside of themselves and take a peep under the hood,
I've learnt to vacate far away from those who bite others back,
When they hear words of advice from people who care for them back,
I've learnt the dreamers and the magic are open to learn,
They listen to others voices and know there's more to grow,
When we are open to receiving help we tell the world we want,
To learn what's here and more to grow instead of resent the ones who don't,
Not everyone is meant to ascend amongst this journey and path,
It might be lonely for a while whilst you shed away the shards,
But then you hit the golden light and soon you will there find,
A palace made from diamond flight upon which you'll delight,
You'll start to mirror in others who know their own worth too,
And everyone will look at you like you've got the magic juice,
You then continue to tell these souls all you've gotta do,
Is bunker down and pop the hatch and look inside of you,
Look at the parts you deem so sad and not worthy of a soul,
To love them, kiss, them, hold them and forgive all their woes,
This magic isn't for the faint of heart but it's for the ones who want,
To manifest all their dreams, desires, beauty and to become strong.
You need to learn that this magic flight will take you beyond your wildest dreams,
Free you from addictions, people, places or things,
That are out of alignment with your best and highest good,
All because you had the courage to take a peep under the hood.

When you make all of your dreams come true,
You remember when you used to,
Be that little girl that was frightened and unaware,
Of her worth and all the demons she had to stare,
Stare at and slay and move away from fast,
Move into the unknown and depart from traumas past,
It's a funny thing to be the child and the adult,
To look back and wish you could have told that little girl,
You're a worth all of the diamonds but not the ones you buy,
The ones that shine deep within you and help you ascend to flight,
Your power is in the knowing that you are not made up of all their sins,
The ones they took and projected on you and you were blind from your kin,
You're a magic piece of art, a beauty and a grace,
You're the worlds counterpart to this divine human race,
You are everything that you could ever want,
All you need to do is look up, lift your head and smile towards the sun,
Your magic stems from deep within,
Like the ghost of Christmas past,
Like New York on a winters night shining from the Christmas Lights,
Like the happiness inside your soul could torch up this earth in flames of delight,
Of divine love and liquid gold and reduce this earths pain,
You hold they key to the castle,
The high vibrational place that you'll call home again,
Everything that aligned with source is all you've ever know,
You'll look back one day and know that this will feel like a past life,
Because everything you are is star dust born of the divine light,
You're magic and you're glorious,
Don't you ever doubt your worth,
You are the only thing on this earth,
Worth a million diamonds and pearls,
So smile my baby girl, You've risen to the top,
You let go of those shackles the ones that you were prisoned with since birth,
Those people were just ones who gave your seed to be born to life,
The genetics that you accrued from them have been reborn through divine flight,
Save your tears and smile babe, You've made it home at last,
You're the most beautiful creature on this earth,
For that I'll make sure you know till the last,
Day you walk upon this earth and go home to the gates,
The pearly ones where nothing feels like anything but golden grace.

The Final Chapter

When the sun finally comes out to play,
And everything that once was all seems grey,
You realise that the journey is not a destination,
But rather a place where you experience life at the universe's station,
The frequency you're tuned into is the the reality you'll be given,
Are you choosing to focus on lack of things flowing in easily given?
Your power is more than you have been told,
Quickly learn and understand it before you get old,
You enjoy to reveal in these heavenly delights,
Whilst you enjoy your youth sailing on a yacht off the coast of Catalina's bite,
You're a beautiful soul with so much to give,
Let go of the trauma and let the light in,
This magic inside of you is all that you need,
It'll orbit around and to you the life of your dreams,
So dream big little baby,
Don't let anyone stop you from your goals,
Anything is achievable no matter what you've been told,
You just have to know it is coming and believe it will show,
Know your worth and your love and focus on the glow,
Glow so bright that you attract things towards you,
Like a lighthouse at sea,
Because your divinity is worth more than the eye can see.

CPSIA information can be obtained
at www.ICGtesting.com
Printed in the USA
LVHW020707300121
677807LV00006B/678